P]

"[*Reckoning*] exhorts readers to confront the worst and ugliest, pleads for progress and peace, and provokes admiration for its resilient, activist author. V shall overcome, someday." —**Alexandra Jacobs, *The New York Times***

"[*Reckoning*] serves as a reflection on the personal, an overview of the professional and a reminder of the political, all with undertones of grief, vulnerability and later-in-life perspective . . . Gutting and gorgeous." —***The Washington Post***

"Bracing . . . V's explosive truth-telling is as provocative as it is intense. The result is a raw and relevant oeuvre." —***Publishers Weekly*** **(starred review)**

"Riveting . . . V digs deep to find the words to constructively address sexual atrocities and everyday sexism and their insidious consequences . . . This far-reaching, deeply affecting collection will garner avid attention and ignite passionate discussion." —***Booklist*** **(starred review)**

"Profound . . . [V] leads by example, plumbing the depths of her memories for the most aching material: her father's abuse; the apathy and agony of her mother; the tumult and pleasures of her past romances; the friendships she has forged across continents; and her life-long struggle to make peace with her own body . . . In its moments of celebration, especially, *Reckoning* is as stirring as a chorus." —***Shelf Awareness***

"Deeply felt, thoughtful, and lyrical, [*Reckoning*] offers a reflection on the connectedness of the personal and political and the need for all humanity to reckon fully with its past in pursuit of a more just world. An elegant and timely book." —***Kirkus Reviews***

"An electric call to heal our broken world." —**Naomi Klein**

"*Reckoning* is a journey from agonizingly personal to utterly cosmic. No reader will be left unshaken and uninspired." —**Jane Fonda**

"For decades, Eve Ensler/V has dared to go where others avert their eyes and their better instincts. That fact, so recognizable in these pages, explains her impact on our era. Happily for the reader, *Reckoning* is part memoir, part manifesto, moving always toward this essential statement: 'Without justice there is no freedom, there is no integrity, there is no full life.'" —**Carl Bernstein**

"Every word, every phrase, every anecdote in this beautiful compilation of V's life's work illuminates. *Reckoning* sheds the searing light of truth on the indignities, falsities, injustices, and cruelties of our world and yet is also a note of love to suffering humanity, revealing and celebrating the fathomless courage and infinite compassion our kind is capable of. A book of true inspiration from beginning to end, emanating from a great spirit and a talent of extraordinary vision." —**Gabor Maté, MD, author of** *The Myth of Normal: Trauma, Illness, and Healing in a Toxic Culture*

"V's *Reckoning* is a phoenix rising from the ashes at the height of her power. What an extraordinary gift to see this woman who refuses to look away, refuses to stay buried, refuses to stay quiet. V stands for many things but perhaps none more so than a woman using the power of a voice that saved her to now save so many others." —**Rachel Louise Snyder, author of** *No Visible Bruises* **and** *Women We Buried, Women We Burned*

"This is a sublime, grand, ferocious, brilliantly written book by one of our most passionate, and illumined, sacred activists. Someone who has dedicated her life to transforming abuse and horror into a clarion call for the renewal of the world. Everyone who is concerned about the future should read this book to be filled with joy, meaning, purpose, and a truth of being that cannot be shaken." —**Andrew Harvey, author of** *The Hope* **and** *Love Is Everything*

"This is an unparalleled exegesis of how we build the political from the personal and how we excavate the personal with the political. If you are trying to find a way to face your deepest hurt in order to be a part of the camaraderie we need to save the planet, open yourself to this rendering." —**Zillah Eisenstein**

RECKONING

RECKONING

V Formerly **Eve Ensler**

BLOOMSBURY PUBLISHING
NEW YORK · LONDON · OXFORD · NEW DELHI · SYDNEY

BLOOMSBURY PUBLISHING
Bloomsbury Publishing Inc.
1385 Broadway, New York, NY 10018, USA

BLOOMSBURY, BLOOMSBURY PUBLISHING, and the Diana
logo are trademarks of
Bloomsbury Publishing Plc

First published in the United States 2023
This paperback edition published 2024

ISBN: HC: 978-1-63557-904-8; PB: 978-1-63973-288-3;
eBook: 978-1-63557-905-5

Library of Congress Cataloging-in-Publication Data is available

2 4 6 8 10 9 7 5 3 1

Designed and typeset by Elizabeth Van Itallie
Printed and bound in the U.S.A.

To find out more about our authors and books visit www.bloomsbury
.com and sign up for our newsletters.

Bloomsbury books may be purchased for business or promotional
use. For information on bulk purchases please contact Macmillan
Corporate and Premium Sales Department at specialmarkets@
macmillan.com.

For the pod—Paula, Celeste, Tony, Alixa, Alia, and Pablo

Saying sorry is not enough . . . A deeper sort of accountability is needed—one that brings us to the edges of ourselves. One that helps us notice that we are a palimpsest of colors, and that who or what we are is always in the making. Forgiveness is settling debts; reconciliation is troubling boundaries.

—BÁYÒ AKÓMOLÁFÉ

AUTHOR'S NOTE

When I use the word "women" in this book I mean for it to be expansive and inclusive.

CONTENTS

INTRODUCTION

This book is about slowing down and assessing and looking, really looking. It's about accountability and discomfort. It's about remembering and honoring the most vulnerable and the most vulnerable moments. It's about lost love, and craving touch in our aloneness. It's about tearing down walls and wondering why we build them. It's about the time of AIDS and a world of endless femicide. It's about grief, trauma, a raging virus, and writing.

It's about reckoning.

I have been blessed to travel the world, to know an astonishing array of scents and accents, to have moved my hips to the rhythms of resistance in many musical languages. I'm not a sightseer. I have spent my days in prisons, theaters, shelters for the unhoused, refugee camps, detention centers, women's centers, cafés, and clandestine locations. There, I have learned the world mainly through the faces, bodies, scars, and stories of women who have suffered the greatest injuries but who still manage to transform their pain into radical action, new forms of leadership, art, gardens, medicine, and healing.

I have never been able to properly separate the personal from the political. I believe, as the great late poet Adrienne Rich once wrote, "The moment when a feeling enters the body / is political. This touch is political."

I have no interest in countries. They are arbitrary demarcations, divisive slashes made by patriarchs on the basis of theft, greed, colonialism, ownership, and violence. Most often they are lands stolen from the Indigenous at the high cost of genocide. I do not have one patriotic bone in my body. I have a serious aversion to flags. They make me nauseous. I blanch at the national anthem or anytime someone says something like "we are the greatest country on earth." I am not a country. My only loyalty is to kindness, dignity, freedom, equality, and life force.

I have always written about the world simultaneously through my body and my brain. I trust my body. I have sharp intuition that evolved out of the need to survive. I am extremely porous. Perhaps I was born this way, or, more likely, the onslaught of abuse at an early age tore open a necessary veil that was meant to protect me from unbearable suffering. Whatever the cause, it has been a blessing and a curse. I have had to learn how to live without an essential layer of skin. For most of my life, I failed at this, eventually growing a cancerous tumor the size of a mango in my uterus. Too much got in. That was thirteen years ago. Since then, I moved to the woods, where I live in the embrace of green, running spring water, massive willows, locust trees, and open sky.

COVID-19 stopped time and simultaneously expanded it. It forced many of us, those who were privileged and lucky and did not have to be on the front lines, to go in, go under. We were locked down with our pasts, our memories, our fears and disappointments, and with the overwhelming tragedies of the world at our fingertips. The virus insisted that we stop advancing, accumulating, adding up. For many of us, particularly theater artists, work, as we knew it, dried up. There was no more theater. That which gave us meaning, value, identity, and a paycheck was suddenly gone. Travel stopped. We couldn't escape our anxiety or ourselves. There was a randomness to it all, like some cosmic game of musical chairs. Wherever you were when the music stopped, whomever you were with, became the pod or the petri dish of your scrutinous metamorphosis.

Before the pandemic many of us lived at the speed of light and ambition. We consumed places, experiences, relationships like snakes swallowing their prey whole. We never chewed or digested. Myself, I moved from country to country, speech to speech, play to play. I had no time to absorb it, reflect, integrate, or understand.

I had no time to reckon. America has never been big on reckoning. Here we live in the always almost about to arrive future. We are a country that is driven by five essential verbs: produce, extract, consume, erase, win. Reckoning and all the attending particulars — like reflection, understanding, and accountability — require an expanse of time and attention. They demand stillness, a stretch of emptiness.

Living in the United States has always felt like living inside a criminal on the run. We are a people running. Running from new house to better house, iPhone to iPhone, state to state, always dissatisfied, always hungry. Running from families, from trauma, from bad feelings, from grief. Running from knowledge and responsibility. Running from the original crime — the guilt and shame of how this country began, stolen from the Indigenous. Running from four hundred years of slavery and all the attending violence and degradation toward Black people.

Living in the United States has always been a breathless

experience. And that was even before the time of COVID, the time when the lack of breath became collectively catastrophic. COVID itself a respiratory virus that put thousands on ventilators and took the final breath from millions worldwide. COVID, the time of a white cop's knee on the neck of George Floyd literally squeezing the breath out of him over nine diabolical public minutes. COVID, the fires in California choking the breath of the earth with smoke—millions of birds suffocating, falling from the sky.

Before COVID, our world was already speeding up, seized by more nimble technologies that drove us, connected us, tweeted us, and canceled us. Our collective body running faster and faster, always the sense that something, someone was nipping at our heels, about to catch us and consume us. And perhaps it finally has. Perhaps COVID slowed things down long enough for our ghosts to fully grab us. I know mine have been out and about all through this involuntary viral retreat.

As this was happening, the world was cracking apart. All that we as a country had attempted to ignore, bury, or deny was glaringly front and center, suddenly magnified and burning. All the inequities, the uncaring, the cruelty at the heart of the U.S. Empire were manifest in real time. We witnessed the ease with which the Trumpian government allowed hundreds of people to become sick and die, then thousands, then hundreds of thousands in a country with all the modern advances and achievements. There was no forethought, no plan, no worry even, nothing to catch or save the dying multitudes who perished so quickly that there was no time to acknowledge or mourn their passing. Due to systemic inequities, Black and brown people were getting the virus at three times the rate of white people and dying twice as fast. Health-care workers were left exposed and unprotected, sent into work wearing garbage bags instead of gowns. Women were used to save us and easily sacrificed. The shattered veins of racist patriarchal capitalism were bleeding everywhere.

COVID ushered in this reckoning full force, and for those who had designed their lives to avoid such a radical confrontation, the virus landed as a shock.

What exactly does it mean to reckon and why is it so critical right now? Reckoning demands remembering, acknowledging, and accounting. It requires a certain humility, a willingness to take stock and look deeply and unflinchingly at what is often right in front of us, but we refuse to see. It means determining both one's personal and collective responsibility and how and when they intersect. And it inherently compels the action of admitting mistakes, apologizing for misdeeds and bad actions, changing course if that's what's required.

For the past forty-five years I have kept journals and diaries. I have stacks of espresso-stained writings. I have written monologues, plays, articles, essays, fables, speeches, rants, and poems. COVID afforded me the time to consider this writing—to trace the map of my lifelong obsessions and curiosities and to gather them into a book of reckoning.

I have done my best to arrange this work thematically rather than chronologically, taking stock, with the trajectory and exigency of reckoning, stripping back layers of denial and defenses throughout.

Reckoning is an anomaly in this age of radical disinformation. It's the antidote to fake news, spinning lies, right-wing attempts to bury our country's disturbing history. We are in the midst of an almost perverse pushback against teaching anything of our true past that might make our children feel disturbed or guilty. This is absurd, infantilizing, and dangerous. We, and our children, will ultimately drown in the polluted sea of diabolical amnesia. It's only in our willingness to face the music, walk through the fire, confront the truth head-on that we are born into ourselves, one another, and a livable future.

This book has been a reckoning with myths and narratives that guided my life and needed revision. It's been a reckoning with loss and contradiction. It's been a reckoning with grief. There is so much unfelt, unshared, unprocessed grief.

In many ways this book is shaped like grief. It's associative and fragmented and out of time. It gathers as it flows. It cares less for logic than heart. It has its own trajectory.

And so, this is also a book about writing.

I have needed to write. It was how I found myself, how I knew I might exist outside the confines of those oppressive and violent forces who had already, at a very young age, determined me to be bad and unworthy. I wrote into an alternative persona and thus initiated a dialogue between the internal and external I that offered agency and identity to the part of myself I will call survivor.

Writing saved me from suicide, from madness. Or at least it made something out of the madness. Writing was witness. It was prosecution, confession, excavation, deliverance. The articulation of words was a kind of bricklaying, building something, even momentarily to stand on, making meaning out of the chaos and violence. I could create beauty. I could find family. For without a mirror of our being, how do we know we exist? The writer Mark Matousek once observed, "You learn the world from your mother's face." But what if her visage is opaque and ungiving? What if she does not have eyes for you, or energy? What world do you find or learn then?

Word by word I eked my way into existence. Each line of a poem, each essay, each play, article, book has been a bulwark against my imminent disappearance. And as you might imagine, an existence built on the accumulation and arrangement of syllables, nouns, and verbs is a most precarious proposition. For the risk, of course, is that the reader will not understand or value or respect what the writer has written, tossing the writer into the fiery and ragged pit of further rejection and loneliness.

One is always failing at writing. One is always one step, one word, away from writing what one actually meant to say. And that gap, that cavern of impossibility, is in some ways more debilitating than any original pain. For it is ongoing proof of one's singular stupidity, incompetence, and failure to make any meaning at all.

Writing is dangerous business. Virginia Woolf descended into depression after she finished each book, believing it was a total failure—until the last book, when after writing it, she walked into a pond with stones in her pocket and never came back. And I would be lying if I did not confess how often I have reread something I have written and felt the desire to mutilate every ounce of my own flesh. I tell myself a rather pathetic tale that one day I will be the writer I dreamed of being. Perhaps this is the single delusion that has kept me going and stopped me from loading my pockets with stones. "This one, this one will be it. When the words match the meaning, the desire, the infinitesimal detail of reality. When I have finally outrun the fissures of memory loss and fragmentation of intelligence wreaked on me as a child through battery and rape. When I have written myself, and my words, back whole and the language has a luminous specificity and reeks with divine grace and clarity. This next one will be the one."

But I am almost seventy now. Time is running out. Someone once said you have to be madly grandiose to write, to believe others would truly be interested in your thoughts. But it could also be that writing is survival. A way of cornering the mess, refusing to be swept away in another's tyranny, a cry in the dark.

We do our best. Uttering as close to the bone as possible.

Venturing further and further into the dark room of truth calling us to be its accomplice. Saying what every cell in our body urges us not to say. Breaking through the guardrails, taboos, and the thorny unspoken.

Including admitting here on the page that at my core for much of my life, I have felt like nothing. Absolute nothing. Reckoning with the knowledge that these years on earth have been perhaps a heroic and often-failed attempt to come from nothing—to unwrap the bandages around my head and, instead of finding air and absence, discover substance and value.

I am older now. Irrelevant in the cult/ure of youth, followers, and TikTok. But I write anyway. I write and write through the last vestiges of night and then suddenly, the sun, igniting the crystal-edged branches of winter trees, diamond starlight flashing against the cerulean sky. I am here and not here. Disappearing and finally gone. And maybe the deepest reckoning is that nothingness that I have feared forever is not frightening after all. Maybe it's where we come from and the vast welcoming emptiness calling us home. And maybe what I have called existence is just the burning desire to grab hold of the others here, now, before I go.

Words Were Burning

1993

When I was ten years old, I asked my father if I could go and play with my best friend, Judy. We lived on the same block and I loved her passionately. My father said no. I asked why. He said, "Because I said no." He was angry that I asked why. Why was his least favorite question. I was visibly disappointed. He told me to smile. I said I didn't want to smile; I didn't have anything to smile about. He said I had better smile. He said it louder. I didn't smile and he struck me across my face, and I went flying across the room and landed hard against the wall. I remember being very surprised, like a bomb going off next to you surprised. I remember that I smiled then, this idiot puppet smile that hurt my cheeks.

I remember this moment because it was the moment that violence passed into me. This was the moment that my trust started to unravel, the moment I became afraid, the moment I had to pretend to be someone else in order to survive. This was the moment that I became the enemy. I lived like a prisoner after that in my father's house. All the landmarks of home—trust-safety-comfort—were gone. I lived like a refugee.

It was in this landscape, in the empty desert, that I gradually and miraculously discovered this other part of me. It wasn't tangible, something you could prove, identifiable. It wasn't attached to the world of my father. He could not touch it or change it. It was bigger than violence or place. It was stronger than his blame or misery. It was smarter than his doubt. It was desire. It was mine.

I discovered this part through words. Words were my friends. Words were little trains traveling through a lush countryside. Words were burning. Words were power. Words were opening windows. Words were taking off my clothes. Words were scheming. Screaming. Resist.

I
WALLS

I have always been obsessed with walls—who needs to build them, who's devoted to tearing them down. Walls. Borders. Closed Doors. What goes on behind them? Prisons. Shelters for the Unhoused. Nuclear Depots. Detention Centers. Suburban Homes. For much of my life I have tried to find ways to get inside.

I volunteered for nine years at a shelter in New York City, working with unhoused women, and for eight years, at Bedford Hills Correctional Facility, facilitating a writing group for women who were doing time for violent crimes. I interviewed women in refugee camps in Pakistan and the former Yugoslavia. I listened to migrant women on the southern border of the United States in the freezing cold and in detention centers and shelters in Brownsville, Texas. There I found young women and mothers with babies desperate for a place that would welcome and care for them as they fled violence and poverty brought on by imperialist U.S. wars and climate crisis.

In all these places I hungered to get through the literal walls of buildings, barbed wire fences as well as the fixed and unbending narratives that not only erased unhoused women, incarcerated women, migrant women, refugee women but presented them so inhumanely.

Then, of course, my entire life has been a journey to gradually and carefully tear down the walls in my own psyche—walls I was forced to erect as a child in order to survive severe violence and abuse. To be strong enough to remember what actually happened to me and strong enough to write about it so that it might help me, and perhaps others, get free.

Make Love Not Wall

On the evening of November 9, 1989, the Berlin Wall began to come down.

I knew I had to be there. To witness, to experience this historic accidental moment. There were all kinds of people there from across Germany and the world. They were nicknamed Mauerspechte (wall peckers). They had come with hammers, chisels, and heavy-duty sledgehammers. They were bringing down the wall, chip by multicolored chip. This is from my diary over those days of wall pecking.

I wake up craving salami and the juice of the spotted meat falls into me like octane. The bathroom door is on an angle and you hurt yourself passing through. My lips have cracks like chipped cement and my eyes are graffiti. DIE MAUER.

They're waiting at Brandenburg. High up on watchtowers over-looking East Germany. But no bulldozers come. Guards think of more ingenious photo opportunities. They pose with one an-other, with roses, with candles. We're waiting for the tap dance.

Heinz Sokolowski, forty-eight, was shot on November 25, 1965, while escaping. Children run along the cobblestone beside the wall like carnival ponies, bucking and singing, searching for pieces of wall like Easter eggs. Trees are shedding. They're al-most bare. Military helicopters hover overhead. A group of boys beat another boy with a newspaper. A taxi drives over to the East. When you look through the holes in the wall, it's a strange kalei-doscope chiseled by human pounding. It's stark and humble on the other side. There are no graffiti or empty beer cups or bright camera lights or Benetton clothes or Batman wear. It's empty like a stage. Anything could happen. All day there is a rising river of waiting, but the equipment does not come.

I pull pieces from the wall like stubborn teeth.

At Checkpoint Charlie there's Mickey Mouse painted on the wall. Americans eat sausage drowned in Heinz ketchup.

In the museum a woman lies naked with a slab of concrete between her legs. Barbed wire runs through people's heads. When this comes down, we're going to have to think in other directions than east and west. We're going to look up at the sky and wonder about ozone, and we're going to look in our arsenals and wonder what all these nuclear weapons are doing there. The flags keep waving, but there are no nations. There is a wall and it's coming down.

The bread is stiff like our frozen shoulders, and I ask him to reheat the goulash. The sun disappears as we follow the wall around Hitler's bunker. A dark thing rises, and I feel soot in my mouth. The wall becomes a massive headstone of unmarked graves, and we are walking on the dead. I call M., and his voice is an armchair. I fall into it and clutch the green hotel phone. When we return, there's a moon over Brandenburg and hot wine and beer. A man in black with a perfect moustache plays an organ as a woman dressed as a bear blows whistles and gets the crowd clapping. The Polizei arrive, the more people drink. It's midnight. U.S. anchormen present their stories. We find warm apple strudel in vanilla sauce, and it tastes like my mother loves me.

NOVEMBER 17

She's warm in bed and she smells like onions. We whisper as the moon rises over a frosted kitchen in Berlin. There's always the smell of something burning. It gets in your clothes, and you think you've been cooking lamb over an open grill.

There are huge orange and yellow Gorbachev balloons, his face pressed on the window, where we drink our tea. Diana Ross is singing in a seventies disco café. A dissatisfied guy blowing huge smoke rings leans on a steel counter. A woman bartender has herpes on her mouth. The lines were so long getting into West Germany they stopped checking passports. Here, on the other side, no one is shopping. The East moves steady west like Missouri. If it weren't communism, you'd swear it was the Puritan ethic. The government keeps announcing the revolution, but all that's changed in the eyes of East Germans peering into the windows at Benetton.

At the wall it's an international parade—the sun's a disco light flashing colors of weathered paints, slogans, and graffiti in a freezing breeze. A white-haired woman with a basket and rosy cheeks scrapes off paint as it falls and gathers dust. A tall man rocks and whacks as serious chunks fly about. A guy in plaid scales a jagged crack. His shoe falls off, and his friend puts it back. Whenever anyone begins the hammering, people gather like a chorus around the soprano. It's opera. MAKE LOVE NOT WALL.

We share a salad, cheese, olives, various lettuces, and the vinegar dressing is sweet on our lips. She massages my back on a bench in the center of Berlin.

It's 5:00 P.M. at Woolworth's. We're searching for a hammer and a left-hand glove. It's bright inside and crowded. The East Germans frantically move about with empty orange baskets.

They hold them upside down like hung squirrels. FREE AT LAST. FREE TO BE DEPRIVED AND WITNESS OUR DEPRIVATION. Muzak hangs over these confused shoppers like a rejected visa.

We are drawn in the cold darkness back to the Wall, where the air on the cobblestone numbs our feet. We find a Roma man who has come to his same place every night, and he is pounding till he can fit his body through, pounding till he can sit with the guard on the other side. We stand by him in the wild November night and close our eyes like children do. A shower of rock rains down on us, and it's just the next thing bursting apart.

Ladies

*The eighties under Ronald Reagan's trickle-down economic poli-
cies were a disaster for poor and middle-class people. The United
States was plagued with high unemployment, destruction of af-
fordable housing, deinstitutionalization of mentally ill patients
who were forced onto the streets with no available treatment, profound cuts in welfare. This left many people vulnerable to being
unhoused. Throughout this period there were an estimated two
hundred thousand to five hundred thousand unhoused people in
America.*

*One day I was simply unable to keep walking past so many
hungry, suffering people on my block in Manhattan. Through
the encouragement of my dear friend, Paula Allen, I began to
volunteer at the Olivieri Drop-In Center on Thirtieth Street. My
play,* Ladies, *grew out of my experience there. It was set in the existential landscape of a women's shelter for the unhoused in New
York City and was loosely based on the stories of women I heard
over the next eight years I was there.* Ladies *was performed in 1989
at the Theater at St. Clement's, produced by the Music-Theatre*

Group. Today there are more than half a million unhoused people in the United States. The average unhoused person does not live past fifty. These are monologues inspired by women I met.

NICKIE

It's what happens when you live outdoors for too long. It all runs together like raw scrambled eggs. Each part of you bleeds into the other. Your emotions are like your things shoved into one goddam cheap Woolworth's bag. You don't even know what's in the bag after a while and you stop caring. All you know is it's heavy and you've got to take it everywhere you go, cos there's no place that wants it. No place will let you keep it there. And one night you just say fuck it, fuck the bag and you leave it. And when you go out you come back after two days and it's gone. You act like you're really pissed off. Who did it? Who took my fucking bag? It's got everything. But deep down you're relieved cos it's gone, and after that you're gone, too, in a way, and it feels better. Kind of.

ALLEGRO

They keep sending us to these broken places. I like pretty things just like everybody else. Because I'm poor doesn't mean I don't have taste and feelings. I don't want your dirty garbage hand-outs. I want a home where I can feel elegant and important, where I am not ashamed to invite my friends. The landlord said I should be grateful. It's a roof. Just like the people who drop their old smelly clothes here. I should be grateful. Do they want to wear these clothes anymore? No, they just cleaned out their closets, so they buy new things. Does a landlord want to live in a sewer? No. Don't you tell me to quiet down. All of us have been quiet too long. You put us in respectable homes, and we will be quiet.

I Was a Funny Person Once

One day a very gaunt woman arrived at the Olivieri Drop-In Center. It was as if she had just surfaced from an underground torture chamber. She had cigarette burns all over her arms and legs. Her hair was literally breaking into pieces. She was covered in dust. She was clearly about to die. I grabbed her and rushed her to the emergency room in a taxi. Even in that near-death state she was making jokes about how attractive she was. I could tell she was funny. I wrote this for her.

It's dark where I am. It's gray and timeless and no one comes. The edges are blurred. The edges are holes filled with thick sour mud that smells like sulfur sometimes and period blood and pee. I have not had a clock by my bed for three years. I have not had a bed. Not a stationary bed I can come back to, a soft, welcoming bed. I am big cow meat on a slab. They move me around a lot. They move me from steel tables and cots. Sometimes I'm a slab of cow meat on two hard orange plastic chairs. Sometimes I'm on concrete. Sometimes the flies rest on me and I don't shoo them away. They fuck on me and lay eggs. The eggs burrow into my skin. I feel the bugs and ugly little things hatching out of me. When I touch my hair, it feels like a wig. It feels like dead people's hair feels like after they've prepared it for the casket. There are hair diseases. When I touched my hair yesterday a whole patch of it came out in my hand. It didn't seem like mine, but I could feel a bald space on my scalp. The memories hurt like sharp rocks against my temples. I was a funny person once. I told stories at cocktail parties and people gathered around and their mouths were open and laughing white teeth and they were all excited about me. I was entertaining. I was funny. I wore silk clothes. I read complicated books. I had clean fingernails. I had a wallet and photographs. I had a telephone and cotton sheets. I've stopped speaking out loud here. The words hurt, they hurt as they're coming out of me. They remind me that I'm dirty. They remind me that I've stopped washing. Stopped moving. Stopped longing. The words are like other people, separate from me and they leave me as they come out. I want to keep my words. I want them to stay. They're my only family.

You are scared of me. I see you. Not looking at me. Working hard to not be looking at me. You are afraid that my poverty will contaminate you. Poverty's contagious. I disgust you. You hate my despair. You are repulsed by my suffering. I am the reminder that anything can happen. That our brains are changed by tragedy. That they sometimes snap. I am the reminder that abuse catches up with you. It can make you forget your name. It can make you lose your way. It can make you pee on yourself and not move from the warm wetness because it feels safe and somewhere else.

600

I am haunted by a letter to the prime minister of Australia and a member of the Australian Parliament written and signed by six hundred asylum seekers imprisoned at Manus Island detention camp in Papua New Guinea. These are people who were trying to get to Australia by boat from countries where they were persecuted. They were caught by the Australian navy and taken to remote islands where they have been held for years with absolutely no way out and no legal recourse.

Hello Dear Mr. Malcolm Turnbull and Peter Dutton,
As the refugees and asylum seekers trapped in Manus Island detention we would like to request you something different this time.

As previously we wrote and asked for help and there was no respond to our request to be freed out of detention we realized that there are no differences between us and rubbish but a bunch of slaves that helped to stop the boats by living in hellish condition.

The only difference is that we are very costly for the Australian tax payers and the Politicians as our job to "stop the boats" is done.

We would like to give you some recommendations to stop the waste of this huge amount of money ruining Australian's reputation and to keep the Australian boarders safe forever.

1. A navy ship that can put us all on board and dump us all in the ocean. (HMAS is always available)

2. A gas chamber (DECMIL will do it with a new contract)

3. Injection of a poison. (IHMS will help for this)

This is not a joke or a satire and please take it serious.

We are dying in Manus gradually, every single day we are literarly tortured and traumatized and there is no safe country to offer us protection as DIBP says.

Best regards
Merry Christmas in advance
Manus refugees and asylum seekers.

I keep thinking what it means that six hundred people wrote a letter requesting to be murdered by a government—how desperate, how decimated, how devalued, how tortured they must have been to make such a demand. Six hundred. That's the number of seats in a jumbo jet.

I am trying to imagine what it feels like not to be wanted anywhere. Anywhere.

To have fled rapes and killings and witnessed the death of the people dearest to you, leaving the house you grew up in, the fields that you know by heart, the view of the mountains or sea that occupy a place in your consciousness that is all you have ever known as home. What it must feel like to be treated like a convict for arriving. For the simple act of arriving. I keep thinking about how easily six hundred people are disappeared, forgotten, destroyed. The extremity of our times—the depth of cruelty and suffering, the psychotic unkindness. The trajectory of the world moves toward criminalization rather than care, punishment before refuge. I keep thinking of Mahmud, the man who wrote the first draft of the letter, who said it was the only letter he ever circulated at the camp that people enthusiastically responded to. The group that collaborated on the letter, adding the various methods of how they wanted to be killed, some wanted to be drowned, some gassed, some just shot straight out. The Muslims in the camp lined up to sign the letter after prayer. What must it feel like to be held on an offshore island in the middle of nowhere in horribly cramped quarters with one thousand traumatized abandoned men and young boys in unbearable heat with no water or medicine, being beaten and harassed and hated, living in the permanent stench of stifling heat and sweat and finding snakes in your room and being flooded when it rains?

The refugees fled Afghanistan, Sri Lanka, Iraq, Iran, Darfur, Syria, Pakistan, and it took searching through at least seven articles to find even a mention of their origins. Imperialist governments bomb and desecrate the bodies of thousands, then they come to hate those who escape and survive as reminders, and then after, spend their days demonizing and destroying them further.

I keep thinking of hundreds of thin half-naked bodies after weeks on a hunger strike, the dried blood on their mouths from where they sewed their lips shut or the others who swallowed razor blades and how these blades must have sliced through their organs and muscle.

I am thinking of the severe anxiety and existential despair of living in endless uncertainty and how boredom can become a mind-breaking torture. There was Reza Barati, a very handsome young man from Iran whose skull was crushed when he was kicked to death in the riots that broke out. I can't stop looking at his picture.

All week I have been with the men and boys on Manus Island. I read their letter over and over. Sometimes I just stare out at the naked trees. Sometimes I cry in the shower. It is not making their pain go away. I know that. It is not freeing them to safety and refuge. I know that. But I will read their letter.

II
AIDS

It happened so quickly. Suddenly scary thin, struggling to breathe or walk, blood brandings on their tender cheeks—falling like ash trees in the greenest of their prime.

It was so particular whom the virus went after—the outrageous ones, the fragile ones, the ones who had never been welcomed, the ones with magic on their tongues, the ones who loved to fuck, the ones whose desires dissolved boundaries and lit up the night. Suddenly like a massive hole in the cultural ozone, they were gone.

Terrorist Angel

NEW YORK CITY, 1997

For almost fifteen years in the eighties and nineties, I had the privilege and joy of coediting a literary magazine called Central Park *with Stephen Paul Martin and Richard Royal. Through the last years of our collaboration Richard was battling AIDS. He had a wicked sense of humor with little tolerance for sentimentality. This was written for him.*

It stopped raining today Richard. The trees had little buds. I will not write a poem about it. I promise you. You were very tall Richard. You made fun of poets who wrote about the weather. Your face would get red and sometimes spit would come out. There is no poetry you would say not since Auschwitz not since Hiroshima. There is no poetry Richard. Not since your body . . .
too boney
to sit on
the toilet
waiting for the shakes
IV with his lunch

his dinner, his happiness
his yellow practical
invisible killer of germs and ulcers
IV where he tripped because his legs
are rubber
and gave out
and the blood spurted
against the tile wall

It stopped raining today Richard. There are sick Kurds knee
deep in freezing mud. Their dead bodies aren't even covered in
shallow graves. We took a walk last spring, you and I, Richard.
We went to the river and you were TB tan. Your head was shaved
and when you laughed, your brain ached. I held your arm and
your elbow cut into me. You planned to come out of the hospital. I read the paper to you. The war was just beginning. We were
sending troops. The cost of every scud missile was your potential
survival. Every tank was a possible cure. The money is gone now
Richard. So are you.
We took him for his last ride
the corridors beige and musty
a lounge chair on wheels
past the rooms of emaciated torsos
past the rooms of wailing lovers
as the game shows played on.

Richard, I pressed sea glass on your chest and dreamed the virus
was leaving you.
I rub the sweetness of his flesh
and know his entire life has been
waiting for his life to begin.

He's hurt. He longs for an appetite.
He asks about mine. I describe
falling in love and its sharp
needles
in places he's already put to sleep.
He's forty-one.
He keeps falling so the nurses tie him to the bed.
He surrenders to the grogginess
The way he once surrendered
in the back of porno stores
in the bushes
in the alleyways

Richard your death is an obscenity. You weren't ready. You
didn't invite it. It wasn't spiritual. Queers do not secretly want to
die. Intercourse isn't evil. Promiscuity doesn't naturally lead to
this. You were an angel Richard. You were a terrorist, and you
were my friend. You were gentle and too angry, and it should
never have come to this.

When he woke up
the oxygen tube had slipped out of his nose.
He checked his penis underneath
the diapers to see if he was peeing,
to see if there was pee.

It stopped raining today Richard. The trees had little buds. I did
not write a poem about it.

All of Us Are Leaving

Every morning at five A.M. Sheila puts bitter melon herbal treatment in her rear end.

Mark is not worrying about caffeine.

Paul feels relieved by the catheter.

Tim is gaining weight.

They were sitting in the candlelight. My friends.

Around my kitchen table.

Mark visits an avatar of the Divine Mother. She holds his head in silence. He has no self-pity.

Sheila has lived with her mother for a year but doesn't tell her about the virus because her mother is a crack addict, and it would upset her.

Paul feels like a fish. His peripheral eyesight is gone, and he can only swim straight ahead. His legs are fins. The branches on the city streets keep bumping into him.

Tim is a powerful city council person, and he uses the word *condom* every chance he gets.

Sheila bought a big winter coat because the cold air is plutonium. It gets through everything.

Mark's body is sculpted and lean. When he wears white, the angels keep flying out of him.

The floor of Paul's studio apartment is the Hudson River. The hypodermic needles, medication packets, and junk food wrappers have washed up on it.

When Sheila teaches in school, the kids think she's pregnant because the fibroid tumors are so swollen inside her.

AZT. DDL. CMV. Can't we just try it?

Paul remembers dark dirty sex on his linoleum floor. He hasn't touched another body since he was diagnosed. He craves sex the way foreigners crave their original language.

Tim makes his boyfriends leave when they look too deeply at him. He has many appointments and is only attached to the telephone.

Paul has another transfusion. He vomits right after the new blood comes in.

Toxic/Macrobiotic. Just eat the pudding.

Mark brings an African violet. He needs to talk after sex about his feelings and is tortured by his lover's silence.

Sheila's only told two people in seven years. She does not go out. People think she's angry with them or bitter about her career. When she used to sing, you could hear the wind blow on the island.

Tim dreams about running for president, but he gets caught having anal sex with a communist.

Paul wakes up and the medication is all gone from the bag. He thinks he's in the ocean and he's gasping for air.

He can't remember why his mother isn't there.

Mark was told by his mother that everything has to do with his penis, mainly the size of it.

It should never have come to this.

Inside my blood.

At my table.

Tim is running for another term.

Mark is not afraid.

Paul is screaming about the triangles of sight that disappear without warning.

Sheila is sleeping.

T-CELLS, FALLING. BITTER MELON REMEDY.

Paul craves sherbet. It soothes the thrush.

Mark isn't worried about caffeine.

Tim eats McDonald's on the run.

Sheila eats only grains and greens.

No one has PCP.

COLD SORES.

I would have held you then.

Mark goes to the gym. He keeps pumping and looking, looking and pumping.

Paul can't get out of the tub.

Sheila's T-CELLS are climbing.

Tim has lost his voice again from shouting.

Paul gets another transfusion. Then all his friends buy him a TV
and a VCR, and he gets excited by *I Love Lucy*.

Mark is talking about the soul. He's talking about the miracle
everyone's searching for that's already here.

HIV is not an identity.

T-CELLS are not the only measure of inevitability.

We keep counting.

Paul is loudly quoting Chekhov.

Tim is angry in front of City Hall. He is throwing sticky purple
condoms, but he'd like to be throwing boulders.

Sheila dreams that she's been asked to give a solo piano concert.
As she plays, she sweats buckets of water, which turns to blood,
which turns to something that looks like Thanksgiving gravy.
Then when people in tuxedos are trying to move away, Sheila
realizes it's all her shit, her whole life of it, and she's happy suddenly, floating ducks and boats and wooden things in it.

Mark doesn't dream anymore. When he closes his eyes, yellow
light surrounds his heart and penis. He laughs when he feels the

creator's hand on him. He laughs like he did once before, before he was seven, before his father left him.

Because they craved connection.

Because they longed to be touched.

Tim is getting handcuffed by a big man wearing rubber medical gloves. "Thank you for protecting me," he says, smiling sexy at the cop like he's about to give him head.

Paul calls me on the phone. His voice is breaking. He asks me with a newborn need if I'll come right over.

In a letter Mark recently wrote me, "I am monstrously impatient inside, full of rage at the incapacity to go deeply enough, passionately enough."

Those that fucked the hardest were in search of it.

Tim is waving from the paddy wagon to his constituents. He notices his cheek is bleeding and tries to cover it.

The virus is passed through semen, blood, and mother's milk. The virus is passed through us.

A huge herb pill is stuck in Sheila's throat. She imagines choking and never coming out of it. And dying and never singing. She got it when she went back to him for one night after seven years. Choking because it stuck in her. Never singing. Throat. Because he was safe, she thought. He was her husband. He was familiar.

I hold Paul, and his head is banging on my shoulder as the big sea fish tears rock out of him. I am the midwife, birthing him into the reality of his death. His denial is the placenta that afterward passes through me.

Is it as devastating as it seems, or is it because I know them?

Around my table. Inside my house.

I force Sheila to stay for tea.

I give Tim some more bean salad.

I bring Paul Fig Newtons.

Mark is eating from the pan.

Mark is eating from the sky, devouring stars, swallowing night.

Sheila is howling at the streetlight that could have been the moon.

Tim is trying to get others through.

Paul is wearing Chinese slippers and they are damp from where his fins are leaking.

All of us are counting now.

All of us are leaving.

Extraordinary Measures

NEW YORK CITY, 1999

The play Extraordinary Measures *was inspired by the final days of my dear friend Paul Walker, an extraordinary theater director, performer, and instructor who died of AIDS in 1993. The play, first performed by Celeste Lecesne at HERE theater in New York City in 1999, presents death as the ultimate class in life study. The hospital room in which Paul lies unconscious, kept alive by medical support systems (the "extraordinary measures" of the title), becomes a forum in which his brother, friends, and former students individually address the man, struggling to find emotional truth before a mentor who can no longer confirm or question their feelings. In the excerpts from monologues below, Paul speaks to us from inside a coma.*

Paul

Where are they? Where are they? I can't find them goddamnit. (He looks under things, throws things around.) Can't see. Can't find them. CMV. No medication. Chunks of sight, triangles of eye space, boxes of vision gone, where are my glasses, need my glasses, can't read without my glasses. Can't see. Someone help me. Dammit help me. (He finds glasses. Sits and calms down momentarily, then it occurs to him that he still can't see.) Can't see. Can't see. Glasses don't help. Can't wake up, can't open the opening part. Can't come back. Can't get through. I keep waking, attempting to wake up inside, and again I am waking inside something already different, already gone. Keep attempting to wake up and be eyes open. Eyes there. Eyes inside this room. Literal room. Eyes inside body, inside bed, inside room. Keep opening my eyes. My eyes aren't like that anymore. Not eyes. I see you eyes. Can't see them. Can't talk, but they're there. Three realities away. I keep waking, wake up. Wake up. Trying to get back. Can't hear me (he screams) I'm in here. I'm stuck in here. Wake up. Can't breathe. Something breathing me. Something massive and thick. Something pushing air in and out of me. Can't breathe. Can't wake up. Can't get back. Caught. Caught.

Caught. Want life. Want breathing. Want air. Want sunlight on dirty hospital windows, want red jello melting in my sore thrush mouth, want Sayaka's hair right after it's permed, Audrey, Audrey, want Audrey, want an audience; hello, hello, don't you see me, won't you see me, so kind of you to come, want the alphabet; A, B, C, D, want my two most recent favorite words; trajectory and limestone, want rice pudding, mash potatoes, *I Love Lucy*, I love Lucy, James Joyce, pentamidine, water towers, *Breakfast at Tiffany's*, want loud annoying birds, Irish rain, Irish wool, want anything I can see, anything green, Terry! Want to be there in the room with you, want to touch, feel your rough winter skin, want my friends, want to wake up. Wanna wake up. Wanna wake up . . . (Mother's voice to calm himself) Keep swimming Paul. Keep swimming. Straight ahead.

Paul

I loved big men. Big full sized Irish men. Men with big hands, strong backs, a little belly. Men who worked the docks, or drove school buses, firemen, men who lifted heavy things all day. Men who worked. Men who in their own small way, kept the world moving forward. Men who were lonely and said so after a couple of drinks. Men who needed to push you against the wall in the dark or flatten you against the worn linoleum floor and have you and hurt you a little because the hunger for having became too much and they raged at themselves for being so needy. Men who were mute, unable to articulate their confusion or vulnerability, who unlike women of the same order, had no capacity for pain or aloneness. These men spoke to me. Their whiskey breath sometimes cursing me in the dark, their massive freckled shoulders pinning me down. Their rough hands gently stroking my hair as they thrust their fear, their ignorance, and doubt into me. I let myself receive their sorrow and frankly, was wild with the receiving, wild with their manly frenzy. I craved their working hands and mouths, their muscular hips and thighs. I craved their erect lonely pricks. I craved them tearing me apart, ripping into the center of my torso, charging into my heart. These men, these big mute working men, opening to me in the dark.

My mother gave me wonder, but not comfort. So, I confused mystery with anonymity, performance with connection, and awe with love.

For Richard

NEW YORK CITY, 1997

Your tears come
to you now
at once like hungry dogs.
The world's on fire.
They keep taking away your future
like your driver's license.
They don't want you back on the road.
Statistics: live barbed wire
around your genitals.
And you, who no longer separate
the red heart
from the breaking one,
you, whose living they can't explain
you grow unmistakably
solidly round
like Buddha.

III

MOTHER HUNGER

They say mother hunger isn't a pathology but an injury. A wound. A hole in the very center. No blame really. Just fact. I needed her milky breasts. I got cigarette smoke instead. I needed her to not let him do that to me. She became his accomplice.

My birth was a disappearance. I became one of the missing. Words were breadcrumbs in the forest—writing my way home, writing to open the gates, to crack the mother code.

I had a shrink who once told me that I spent my life pasting on the arms of my lovers so they would be able to hug me.

Consider my words glue.

Dear Mother

JOURNAL ENTRY, 1994

I am afraid of my belly button. I cannot touch it. Once I imagined it unraveling outside me, and the cord, infinite in length, wrapping itself around my enemies. Another time I saw it falling off inside me like a poisonous tablet rushing through the bloodstream. I turned all kinds of colors. I died. There was no heaven, just this heartbeat without a body.

Mother, I am afraid of the death inside me. It stretches out like long flatlands with no horizon.

I am asking you kindly to move back into your own country.

My Mother Was Not
My Mother

NEW YORK CITY, 2000

My mother was not my mother
I was the property of my father. I was his thing.
Like a chair.
Like a dried leaf.
Like a broken telephone.

My mother and I never bonded.
I don't remember her body.
I don't crave her breasts.
I would not find her instinctively in a crowd.

When I was forty, we had our first conversation.
My father was dead then.
We were relaxed.
It took me until I was forty-two to begin to see my mother

through my eyes
and not my father's.

My mother is funny.
She does a singing-whistling thing when she is by herself.
It would have become a dance
if she had been happy.

She is thin.
After she had lung cancer and they took a lung,
her breasts shrunk and now
she can wear dresses that are too tight for me.
We have the same body.
It is a body that doesn't gain weight.
Except later a little in the stomach.
It is a body that gets skinny when it gets old and sick.
It is athletic.
It needs to move.

My mother and I both like to sleep late.
The early morning makes us feel suicidal.
There is no veil, and it hurts so early.
We are night birds.
It's past midnight now and she's still awake in her room.
Before I would have been paralyzed in her loneliness.

I always thought my mother was a coward.
I had contempt for her.
She watched me get beaten.
She watched me get bloody noses in restaurants.
She never protected me.

She told me it was my fault.
She didn't leave my father.

My father was seventeen years older than my mother.
He had money and he made her feel stupid.
She had his babies.
I was one of them
But I was his thing
Like a sharp pencil.
Like a torn map.
Like an empty glass.
I did not have a mother.

When I was forty-two my mother put aloe on my sunburn.
I think I burned myself so she would touch me.
She was so tender
I think we were both surprised.
I felt for the first time that she liked me.
I wanted to cry.
I didn't mind her smell.
I saw that she was kind.

When I was thirty-nine, I told my mother that my father raped me.
It was raining and there was a big sea storm.
All the roads were flooded.
My mother wanted to leave the room
but she didn't
we watched something getting free.

Next morning, she called me at six A.M.
I knew this was extreme because she does not get up early.

She was weeping
and she knew it was true
I had betrayed her, and she had betrayed me
and we didn't even know each other.
Right then we stopped being other people's property.

The next day we visited the wounded bird museum
In Sarasota Florida
It was overcast and a big pelican was limping.
Most of the birds were broken.
They would never fly again
or leave their wounded bird cages.

Months later my mother called and asked
what she would do if my father came to her
after she died and was mad at her
because she believed me over him,
what if he felt betrayed?
I said my father was dead.
But I could feel him too.

My mother buys me things and we spend his money
And we are filled with this wild, frenzied glee.

Sometimes she still speaks his opinions.
I know because she's usually had a few cocktails.
Her face changes and she looks angry like him.
I don't like her then or I don't
like what she's saying.

I think my mother is proud of me.
I think she is happy alone.
It is calm, quiet not violent where she lives by the sea.
There are other widows by the pool
and she is wild for the pelicans.

How Fragile

DREAM, MAY 15, 1998

I was so tired from the dream. It felt like a hard ball was lodged in my brain. I could feel I was losing my mother the way you lose hair or time or body parts. I was trying to get out, fighting my way through that tight opening, the blood, the labia, the juice of my mother. Fighting to say I begin here. You end there.

In the dream I told my ex–best friend she couldn't come back into my life even if she was pretty and petite and unbearably seductive and mean without being mean and me without ever being me and out to win. I screamed in the dream that we had made a boundary, a decision, a line, and she couldn't cross it 'cause every time she crossed it, I disappeared. She couldn't cross it. I noticed I was screaming in the dream and she was breaking, fucking breaking. I couldn't believe it. How fragile. How thin, how without substance, unformed, how not what I had created her to be.

The Whole World Is Raining

DREAM, 2012

I started to dial my mother, but I haven't had a dial phone in fifteen years and my mother is dead.

Last time I called like that I was drunk. I was around twenty-two or so, sloppy in some sleazy Manhattan bar, crying about how the whole world was raining.

I could hear my father in the background screaming for my mother to hang up. She did. She never called back. To see.

Battered Baby

This monologue was commissioned by Molly Smith at the Arena Stage for a production in October, 2022 called My Body, No Choice.

When my mother died, she left me a thick, dark-brown envelope strapped tightly with elastic ties. The ties felt like they were holding something in—a sinister energy, perhaps, or one of those explosive secrets that changes the trajectory of your life. I had no desire to find out. I did not touch that package for years. It sat gathering dust in a basket out of sight. When I would occasionally stumble upon it, I would immediately feel ill, a sense of imminent doom.

To be honest, receiving the package had surprised me. It never occurred to me that my mother thought about me, let alone had collected cherished relics of our shared history. This envelope was the only thing she had specifically left for me.

Then one day it just happened. I hadn't planned it. I didn't realize until later that it was the anniversary of my mother's death. I am not the kind of person who keeps track of those things.

I just took the package out of the basket, undid the ties, and opened it. It had a funny smell. Like pain. Does pain have a smell? Everything felt old and fragile as if my touch could disintegrate it. It was a strange collection: my fifth-grade report card (why fifth grade?), sentimental Mother's Day cards I had given my mother—cards with cats, rainbows, butterflies, tragic poems full of contrition and fake emotion—my birth certificate, a blurred social security number, a program from my college graduation, my commencement speech typed and hardly legible on onionskin paper, and my final grades at college. There were some desperate drunken letters sent after I graduated when I'd clearly already lost my way.

There was a strange assortment of photographs—me, receiving my diploma in a gown and hippie sandals, me and my mother sitting on my bed under an orange Indian print material looking strikingly uncomfortable. Some childhood shots—one I vaguely remember posing for. My father had hired some fancy NY photographer. The "shoot" was agonizing and went on forever. My hair had been permed. I look catastrophically cute. There are profile shots where even my petite nose could not conceal that I was Jewish; alert eyes with sorrow right around the edge, a little cloth strawberry pinned to my white pinafore dress. A note, written on my father's stationery, was attached to the photos expressing his great disappointment in the photographs, "These photographs do not remotely resemble the children I know." I felt bad for the photographer. I knew what it felt like to disappoint my father.

At the very bottom of the stack was a picture that stopped my heart. I had to look a few times. Yes, it was definitely me as a baby, but I was a battered baby. Two black eyes, bruises over my eyebrows, a bloody slash across my nose. I looked like a thug, a baby thug. A battered thug baby.

Up until that moment I had all kinds of theories to account for my great aversion to babies. Everything about infants felt sad and terrifying and everything about having one myself felt treacherous and suffocating. I would surely break one or accidentally hurt it, forget to feed it, leave it outside. I had constant nightmares of arriving somewhere after a long journey and realizing I had left my baby on the train or in the woods or dropped it along the way without noticing.

I would invariably make this baby sad because all I knew of babies was that they were sad. And I did not want a sad baby.

Babies destroyed your perfect figure, turned your body and brain to mush. They were annoyances, something that interrupted cocktail hour; loud things; demanding, messy, pissing, snotty, pooping things. My mother hated mess and particularly poop. She had toilet trained me by leaving me in the same pair of soiled diapers for over a week. Sad dirty battered thug baby.

By five years old, right around the time my father began to molest me, I knew I would never ever have a baby. When other girls were dressing and coddling and cooing their baby dolls. I was beheading mine, cutting off their hair or drowning them in the rough ocean.

And then of course there was the question: Why had my mother included this photograph in the envelope? What was she trying to tell me? Was she letting me know that what I thought to be true was actually true? Why hadn't she shown it to me when she was alive? Why had she kept this picture? Did she take it? How often did this battery happen? Who did it to me? My brother, with a truck at my forehead; my father, later he beat me regularly; did my mother drop me or let me wander off a ledge?

Why did it all suddenly feel so familiar, like someone was always coming at me, at my body, at my face? I spent an entire childhood ducking, fists permanently raised like a boxer, quick but never fast enough, darting, panicked, frenetic, unbearably anxious. My body was never my body. Pressing cold washcloths on the sting of a hard slap. Covering choke marks on my throat with turtleneck shirts and sweaters. Holding my face where my mother would thunk her middle finger and thumb on my cheek hard. Hard. It really hurt—leaving a vibrating red mark. But it humiliated more than it hurt as it felt like she was flicking off shit. I was the shit.

When exactly did this body, this face stop being mine and become a field for violence and disgrace?

And, of course, I started drinking and smoking and drugging and putting anything into this body that might take the pain, numb the pain, the threat of pain, the memory of pain away. I started at fourteen.

And, of course, the drinking and drugging took me out of my body, away away from the source of the pain, but away from myself as well, away from consent and stop and no, and who are you and I don't really want to and please stop—away from choice. This body that no longer belonged to me, that had long ago become a broken thing, a hurt sad thing, an object to be battered, smacked, ravaged, taken, fucked. This body, public property, his property becoming their property and then suddenly out of this fog, this hangover, the doctor announced that I was pregnant. It happened like that for so many of us. Pregnant. Filled with the horror of sad baby. My life suddenly over before it started. Caught, strangled, oh no, oh God no no no how could I be pregnant? It never occurred to me that there was any life left inside me.

I was suddenly filled with anxiety, a growing body of unbearable about to blow my brains out anxiety, a doom so vast, so enormous I felt consumed, had to lay on the floor. Heart stopping, can't breathe anxiety. Please God, even though I don't believe in you, please God, don't make me have this baby. Take this doom.

And I was somehow saved. That abortion, that day of salvation. July 4. They removed that growing swallowing doom from my body.

I was trembling. The doctor was kind. There was a nurse who held my hand. I remember the sound of a vacuum suctioning. I remember falling through time.

Later I got a bottle of gin and some tonic and lime and ice. I remember lying in bed in the halfway house where I was living in a tiny room. I had always despised July 4, but for the first time, the fireworks nearby were sounding my bodily autonomy and liberation, and not a world war. I toasted each explosion and toasted my naked body in the mirror. I toasted each cramp and I rejoiced in the blood. I bowed to whatever forces had spared me.

This abortion was the first real choice I had ever made about my own body. I was twenty-three. My body that had been battered, raped, denigrated, and taken by clumsy aggressive boys in the dark. My body that had been erased, that had felt so dead, was suddenly empty and alive.

Dear White Women

2018
___

This piece was written for Time *magazine during the Brett Kavanaugh confirmation hearings for Supreme Court Justice.*

Dear white women who support Brett Kavanaugh for Supreme Court Justice,

Last night when I saw Donald Trump mock Dr. Christine Blasey Ford at a speech he was giving to thousands, I couldn't help focusing on the women behind him who cheered and laughed. I felt like I was falling into a familiar nightmare. It compelled me to reach out to you.

When I was a child my father sexually abused and beat me. My mother did not protect me. She sided with my father, just like these women sided with Donald Trump, and I understand why. She sided with him because he was the breadwinner. She sided with him because of her need to survive. She sided with him because the reality of what was happening in front of her was so terrible, it was easier not to see.

She sided with him because she was brought up never to

question a man. She was taught to serve men and make men happy. She was trained not to believe women. It was only much later, after my father died, that she was able to acknowledge the truth of my childhood and to ask for my forgiveness. It was only then, too late, that she was able to see how she had sacrificed her daughter for security and comfort. She used those words. I was her "sacrifice."

Some people, when they look at this video of women laughing at Dr. Ford, will see callousness. I see distancing. I see denial. I have worked on ending violence against women for twenty years. I have traveled this country many times. I have sat with women of all ages and political persuasions. I remember the first performances of my play *The Vagina Monologues* in Oklahoma City, when half the women in the audience came up to tell me they had been raped or battered. Most of them whispered it to me, and often I was the first and only person they had told. Until that moment, they had found a way to normalize it. Expect it. Accept it. Deny it.

I don't believe you want to have to choose your sons and your husbands over your daughters. I don't believe you want the pain that was inflicted on us inflicted on future generations.

I know the risk many of you take in coming out to say you believe a woman over a man. It means you might then have to recognize and believe your own experience. If one out of three women in the world have been raped or beaten, it must mean some of you have had this experience. To believe another woman means having to touch into the pain and fear and sorrow and rage of your own experience and that sometimes feels unbearable. I know because it took me years to come out of my own denial and to break with my perpetrator, my father. To speak the truth that risked upending the comfort of my very carefully constructed life. But I can tell you that living a lie is living half a life. It was only after telling my story that I knew happiness and freedom.

I know the risk others of you face who have witnessed those you love suffer the traumatic aftereffects of violence and those who worry for your children who may someday face this violence.

I write to you because we need you, the way I once needed my mother. We need you to stand with women who are breaking the silence in spite of their terror and shame. I believe inside the bodies of some of those women who laughed at that rally were other impulses and feelings they weren't expressing.

Here is why I believe you should take this stand with me. Violence against women destroys our souls. It annihilates our sense of self. It numbs us. It separates us from our bodies. It is the tool used to keep us second-class citizens. And if we don't address it, it can lead to depression, alcoholism, drug addiction, overeating, and suicide. It makes us believe that we are not worthy of happiness.

It took my mother forty years to see what her denial had done and to apologize to me. I don't think you want to apologize to your daughters forty years from now. Stop the ascension of a man who is angry, aggressive, and vengeful and could very well be a sexual assaulter. Time is short. Call your senators. Stop laughing and start fighting.

With all my love,

Eve

IV

FEMICIDE

The intentional killing of women and girls and female-identified people.

Rachel's Bed

Sometime in 1993 I was walking down a street in Manhattan when I was seized by a photograph on the cover of Newsday— *five young Bosnian girls who had just been returned from a rape camp. It seemed utterly surreal and impossible. I had to go there. This is from my diary.*

"They took my sixty-year-old mother and sixty-eight-year-old father outside. These Chetniks, these boy soldiers who grew up with us, who went to primary school with us. They made my father stand in the center of our lawn, and they held guns to his head. Then they began to throw stones at him, pelting him in his head, his neck, his groin as he stood helpless and confused before me, my mother, our relatives. He was bruised and bleeding and exposed and they wouldn't stop."

I am sitting in a metal chair in a circle of women, all of whom
are smoking and drinking thick black coffee. We are in a make-
shift doctor's office in a refugee camp outside Zagreb, Croatia,
listening to a thirty-year-old woman "doctress" (as my translator
calls her) describe her recent experiences in Bosnia. It is the
summer of 1994, and I have come here, and later to Pakistan,
for two months to interview Bosnian refugees. Outraged by reports of atrocities committed toward women, I have come as a
playwright and screenwriter to write a film script.

"Then they took my mother and poured gasoline around her
feet. For three hours they lit matches and held them as close
to the gasoline as they could. My mother turned white—it was
very cold outside. For three hours they tortured her. Then she
started screaming. She ripped her skirt open and screamed, "Go
ahead, you Chetniks. Kill me. I am not afraid of you, not afraid
to die. Kill me."

The other Bosnian women seem to have stopped breathing as they listen. I hear myself asking questions, through my

translator, in a strange reporter-like voice that implies I have seen all of this before, that it is just another war story. I ask, "How do you explain your neighbors turning against you like that?" and "Did you ever worry about being a Muslim before the war?" I ask these questions from behind my professional persona, as if it were a secret shield, a place of safety.

"After I had finally escaped and gotten here," the doctor continues, "I heard our village was safe again. The United Nations forces raided the concentration camp, and my father was released. I began to get a glimmer of hope. Then the Chetniks invaded my village. They butchered every member of my family with machetes. My mother and father were found, their limbs spread over our lawn."

I listen to her words and feel something caving in. Logic. Safety. Order. Ground. I don't want to cry. Professionals don't cry. Playwrights see people as characters. She is a doctor character. She is a strong, resilient, traumatized woman character. I bear down on the parts of my body where shakes are escaping.

For my first ten days in Zagreb, I slept on a couch in the Center for Women War Victims. The center was created in 1991 to serve Serbian, Muslim, and Croatian women refugees who had been raped in the war. It now served over five hundred women who not only had been raped but had been made unhoused by the war. Most of the women who work there are refugees themselves. They run support groups and provide emergency aid — food, toiletries, medication, children's toys. They help women to find employment, access to medical treatment, schools for their children.

In those first days, I spent five to eight hours a day interviewing women in city centers, desolate refugee camps, and local cafés. I met a country of women dressed in black—black silk, black cotton, black Lycra. In all the interviews, I either was filled with an overwhelming desire to rescue the women— which rendered me powerless and sometimes resentful—or tried to maintain my playwright position. I was hearing their stories as potential dramas, measuring their words in terms of beats and momentum. This approach made me feel cold, impervious, superior.

Thousands of journalists had already passed through these women's lives. The women felt invaded, robbed, ripped off. It was an honor and a privilege that the refugee workers had brought me into these camps, even at times had focused the groups around my being there. I realized I was not honoring my end of the contract. My ways of relationship were hierarchical, one-sided, based on a perception of myself as a healer, a prob- lem solver—which in turn was based on a desperate, hidden need to control: control chaos and protect myself from too much loss, cruelty, and insanity. My need to analyze, interpret, even create art out of these war atrocities stemmed from my inability to be with people, to be with their suffering, to listen, to feel, to be lost in the mess.

On the tenth day in Zagreb, a woman named Rachel, who worked in the center, offered me her apartment for the week- end. I was terrified. It was the first time I'd been alone since my arrival in Croatia, the first time I'd been able to process the experience, to find out where I really was. It was nighttime when I got there, and the lights in the hallway kept going off, leaving me in utter panic and darkness. In all my years as an activist—working in women's shelters for the unhoused, tying myself to fences in protest of nuclear war, sleeping in outdoor peace camps amid rain and rats, camping on the windy Nevada nuclear test site in radiation dust—I had never felt so lonely. I called the States. I paced the apartment. I tried to read but was unable to concentrate. Finally, I lay down on Rachel's bed, with its splendid red comforter.

My heart, breaking from the inside like an organism miscarrying itself, the stories of cruelty: the lit cigarettes almost put through the soldier's wife's eyeballs, the decapitated heads of her old parents, the fifteen-year-old girl whom her soldier husband and his friends raped in the car, the pistol the soldiers put into her three-month-old baby's hand as a joke, the food they didn't serve the Muslim girl's mother who had decided to give birth to the baby of the Serb who raped her, the Canadian uncle who attempted to molest his fourteen-year-old niece from Sarajevo who had fled to him for safety, the dirty, stained clothes that arrive in boxes of humanitarian aid that the refugee women are supposed to be grateful for.

It wasn't the cruelty, the primitive horror, which broke my heart. What hurt was how I defended myself against my love for the refugees. The woman who made sweet pastry in what was now her kitchen, bedroom, living room, bathroom all in one—made pastry for me, a stranger. The one who kept smiling with missing teeth, who gave strength to the woman next to her who smoked cigarettes, smoothed her skirt, apologized for her messy hair. Tears broke out of my eyes like glass cutting flesh, breaking me, making me no one, no longer concrete, broke through my craving for definition, authority, fame, broke all that into tiny pieces that would not hold, becoming liquid, then nothing I could identify, nothing that resembled me or the matter of me. There was just pulp. Masses of beating, bloody pulp. There was just melting.

After my night in Rachel's bed, my journey was transformed. I began to see my interviews as sacred social contracts. I could not simply take stories, events, feelings from my subjects. There had to be an exchange. I had to be present with them. I had to be vulnerable. I could no longer protect myself, stand outside the stories I was hearing. War was not natural. I would never be comfortable with atrocity and cruelty. I found myself crying often during the interviews. I felt little, helpless. Old defenses, identities, approaches died away.

Melt me. Let me dissolve. Let me release my hard identity. Let me be swallowed by the circle. Let me not matter. Let me be homeless, homesick. Let me be disappointed so I can break more. Let me be anonymous so I can be invisible. Not worrying about my turn, my message, my serving, my creation, my moment. Please make me ready to sit in the circle.

Women Left for Dead and the Man Who's Saving Them

I wrote this piece for Glamour *magazine after my first trip to the Democratic Republic of the Congo. I was invited there by Dr. Denis Mukwege, whom I had interviewed at NYU School of Law. He later went on to win the Nobel Peace Prize.*

I have just returned from hell. I am trying for the life of me to figure out how to communicate what I have seen and heard in the Democratic Republic of the Congo. How do I convey these stories of atrocities without your shutting down, quickly turning the page, or feeling too disturbed?

How do I tell you of girls as young as nine raped by gangs of soldiers, of women whose insides were blown apart by rifle blasts and whose bodies now leak uncontrollable streams of urine and feces?

This journey was a departure for me. It began with a man, Dr. Denis Mukwege, and a conversation we had in New York

City in December 2006, when he came to speak about his work helping women at Panzi Hospital in Bukavu. It began with my rusty French and his limited English. It began with the quiet anguish in his bloodshot eyes, eyes that seemed to me to be bleeding from the horrors he'd witnessed.

Something happened in this conversation, his invitation, that compelled me to go halfway around the world to visit the doctor, who was sewing up women as fast as the mad militiamen could rip them apart.

I am going to tell the stories of the patients he saves so that the faceless, generic, raped women of war become Alfonsine and Nadine—women with names and memories and dreams. I am going to ask you to stay with me, to open your hearts, to be as outraged and nauseated as I felt sitting in Panzi Hospital in faraway Bukavu.

Before I went to the Congo, I'd spent the past ten years working on V-Day, the global movement to end violence against women and girls (cisgender, transgender, and those who hold fluid identities that are subject to gender-based violence). I'd traveled to the rape mines of the world, places like Bosnia, Afghanistan, and Haiti, where rape has been used as a tool of war. But nothing I ever experienced felt as ghastly, terrifying, and systematic as the sexual torture and attempted destruction of the female species here. It is not too strong to call this a femicide, to say that the future of the Congo's women is in serious jeopardy.

This femicide serves the larger project of the continuing economic war on the Congo by the West, the pillaging of their resources and raw minerals: copper, tin, gold, and coltan, which goes into making iPhones and computers.

Women are raped (often in front of their husbands), families and communities are broken, people flee their villages, and the militias, who are proxies for multinationals, gain access to mines. The deadly intersection of endless colonialism, capitalism, and racism is now being fought on the landscape of women's bodies.

Dr. Mukwege picks me up at 6:30 A.M. It is a lush, clean morning. Bukavu, where Panzi Hospital is located, is wildly fertile. There are banana trees and psychedelic birds. And there is Lake Kivu, a vast body of water that contains enough methane to power a good portion of sub-Saharan Africa—yet the city of Bukavu on its banks has only sporadic electricity. This is a theme in the Congo. There are more natural resources than almost anywhere else on the planet, yet 80 percent of the people make less than a dollar a day. More rain falls than one can imagine, but for millions, clean drinking water is scarce. The earth is gorgeously abundant, and yet almost one third of the population is starving.

As we drive along the semblance of road, the doctor tells me how different things were when he was a child. "In the sixties fifty thousand people lived here in Bukavu. It was a relaxed place. There were rich people who had speedy boats in the lakes. There were gorillas in the mountains." Now there are at least a million displaced Congolese, many of whom arrive in the city daily, fleeing the numerous armed groups that have ravaged the countryside since fighting erupted in 1996. What started as a civil war to overthrow the dictator Mobutu Sese Seko soon became "Africa's first world war," as observers have called it, with soldiers from neighboring countries joining in the mayhem. The troops have various agendas: Many are fighting for control of the region's extraordinary mineral wealth. Others are out to grab whatever they can get.

But you have to go back further than 1996 to understand what is going on in the Congo today. This country has been tortured for more than 120 years, beginning with King Leopold II of Belgium, who "acquired" the Congo and, between 1885 and 1908, exterminated an estimated ten million people, about half the population. The violent consequences of genocide and colonialism have had a profound impact on the psyche of the Congolese. Despite a 2003 peace agreement and recent elections, armed groups continue to terrorize the eastern half of the country. Overall, the war has left nearly four million people dead — more than in any other conflict since World War II — and resulted in the rape of hundreds of thousands of women and girls.

In Bukavu the people escaping the fighting walk from early morning to late at night. They walk and walk, searching for a way to buy or sell a tomato, or for a banana for their baby. It is a relentless river of humans, anxious and hungry. "People used to eat three meals a day," says Dr. Mukwege. "Now they are lucky to eat one."

Everyone knows the doctor, an ob-gyn. He waves and stops to inquire about this person's health, that person's mother. Most doctors, teachers, and lawyers fled the Congo after the wars started. It never occurred to Dr. Mukwege to leave his people at their most desperate hour.

He first became aware of the epidemic of rape in 1996. "I saw women who had been raped in an extremely barbaric way," he recalls. "First, the women were raped in front of their children, their husbands, and neighbors. Second, the rapes were done by many men at the same time. Third, not only were the women raped, but their vaginas were mutilated with guns and sticks. These situations show that sex was being used as a weapon that is cheap.

"When rape is done in front of your family," he continues, "it destroys everyone. I have seen men suffer who watched their wives raped; they are not mentally stable anymore. The children are in even worse condition. Most of the time, when a woman suffers this much violence, she is not able to bear children afterward. Clearly these rapes are not done to satisfy any sexual desire but to destroy the soul. The whole family and community are broken."

We arrive at Panzi Hospital, a spread-out complex of about a dozen buildings. Eight years ago, Dr. Mukwege created a special maternity ward here with an operating room. Panzi as a whole has 334 beds, 250 of which now hold female victims of sexual violence. The hospital and its surrounding property have become, essentially, a village of raped women. The grounds are overwhelmed with children and hunger and need. Every day at least two children here die from malnutrition. Then there are the many problems that result from severe trauma: women with nightmares and insomnia, women rejected by their husbands, women who have no interest in nurturing the babies of their rapists, women and children with nowhere to go.

It is early morning, and the hospital courtyard has been transformed into a temporary church. Women dressed in their most colorful, or perhaps only, pagne (a six-yard piece of brightly patterned cloth that can be wrapped into a dress or skirt) sit waiting for the doctor to arrive and lead the prayer service that begins each day. A dedicated staff of female nurses and social workers are there as well, dressed in their starched white jackets. There is singing, a combination of Pentecostal calls and Swahili rhythms, Sunday-morning voices calling up Jesus.

This morning service is a kind of daily gathering of strength and unity. When the women sing, everything else seems to disappear. They are with the sun, the sky, the drums, each other. They are alive in their bodies, momentarily safe and free.

As they sing, Dr. Mukwege tells me stories about the women in the chorus. Many were naked when they arrived, or starving. Many were so badly damaged he is amazed they are singing at all. He takes enormous pride in their recovery. "I will never be ashamed," the women sing. "God gave me a new heart that I can be very strong."

"At the beginning I used to hear patients' stories," Dr. Mukwege tells me. "Now I abstain." I soon understand why. I meet Nadine (like others in this story, she agreed to be photographed, but asked that her name be changed, as she could be subject to reprisals for speaking out), who tells me a tale so horrendous it will haunt me for years to come.

When we begin talking, Nadine seems utterly disassociated from her surroundings—far away. "I'm twenty-nine," she begins. "I am from the village of Nindja. Normally there was insecurity in our area. We would hide many nights in the bush. The soldiers found us there. They killed our village chief and his children. We were fifty women. I was with my three children and my older brother; they told him to have sex with me. He refused, so they cut his head and he died."

Nadine's body is trembling. It is hard to believe these words are coming out of a woman who is still alive and breathing. She tells me how one of the soldiers forced her to drink his urine and eat his feces, how the soldiers killed ten of her friends and then murdered her children: her four-year-old and two-year-old boys and her one-year-old girl. "They flung my baby's body on the ground like she was garbage," Nadine says. "One after another they raped me. From that my vagina and anus were ripped apart."

Nadine holds on to my hand as if she were drowning in a tsunami of memory. As devastated as she is, it is clear that she needs to be telling this story, needs me to listen to what she is saying. She closes her eyes and says something I cannot believe I'm hearing. "One of the soldiers cut open a pregnant woman," she says. "It was a mature baby and they killed it. They cooked it and forced us to eat it."

Incredibly, Nadine was the only one of the fifty women to escape. "When I got away from the soldiers, there was a man passing. He said, 'What is that bad smell?' It was me; because of my wounds, I couldn't control my urine or feces. I explained what had happened. The man wept right there. He and some others brought me to the Panzi Hospital."

She stops. Neither of us has breathed. Nadine looks at me, longing for me to make sense of what she's related. She says,

"When I got here, I had no hope. But this hospital helped me so much. Whenever I thought about what happened, I became mad. I believed I would lose my mind. I asked God to kill me. Dr. Mukwege told me: Maybe God didn't want me to lose my life."

Nadine later tells me that the doctor was right. As she fled the slaughter, she says, she saw an infant lying on the ground next to her slain parents. Nadine rescued the girl; now having a child to care for gives her reason to keep going. "I can't go back to my village. It's too dangerous. But if I had a place to live, I could go to school. I lost my children but I'm raising this child as my own. This girl is my future."

I stay for a week at Panzi. Women line up to tell me their stories. They come into the interview numb, distant, glazed over, dead. I begin to understand that the deepest wound for them is the sense that they have been forgotten, that they are invisible, and that their suffering has no meaning. The simple act of listening to them has enormous impact. The slightest touch or kindness restores their energy. Dr. Mukwege tells me I need to meet Alfonsine (her name also has been changed). "Her story really touched me," he says. "Her body, her case is the worst I have ever seen, but she has given us all courage."

Alfonsine is thin and poised, profoundly calm. She tells me she was walking through the forest when she encountered a lone soldier. "He followed me and then forced me to lie down. He said he would kill me. I struggled with him hard; it went on for a long time. Then he went for his rifle, pressed it on the outside of my vagina and shot his entire cartridge into me. I just heard the voice of bullets. My clothes were glued to me with blood. I passed out."

Dr. Mukwege tells me, "I never saw such destruction. Her colon, bladder, vagina and rectum were basically gone. She had lost her mind. I was sure she wouldn't make it. I rebuilt her bladder. Sometimes you don't even know where you are going. There's no map. I operated on her six times, and then I sent her to Ethiopia so they could heal the incontinence problem, and they did."

"I was in bed when I first met Dr. Mukwege," Alfonsine says. "He caressed my face. I lived at Panzi for six months. He helped me spiritually. He showed me how many times God makes miracles. He built me up morally."

I look at Alfonsine's petite body and imagine the scars beneath her humble white clothes. I imagine the reconstructed flesh, the agony she experienced after being shot. I listen carefully. I cannot detect a drop of bitterness or any desire for revenge. Instead, her attention is fixed on transforming the future. She tells me with great pride, "I am now studying to be a nurse. My first choice is to work at Panzi. It was the nurses who nurtured me day after day, who loved me back into living."

Alfonsine has ambitions that go beyond Panzi: "I feel like a big person in my community; I can do something for my people. Women must lead our country. They know the way."

Every day about a dozen new women arrive at Panzi Hospital. Most come for surgery to repair a fistula, a rip in their internal tissue. There are two types of fistulas seen here: One is the aftermath of brutal rape, the other the result of birth complications, something that could be prevented if there was adequate maternity health care. These obstetric fistulas are the result of abnormal tearing during the birth process. Many occur when women flee the militias while they are in labor; there is no time to give birth, and the baby dies inside. The women who make it here are the lucky ones. They limp on homemade canes made from tree branches; they trudge slowly in deep pain. Some have walked forty miles. Because it takes so long to get to the hospital, women have no chance to receive the anti-HIV medications that must be taken within forty-eight hours after rape. Health experts fear that in a few years, there will be an explosion of AIDS in the Congo.

Dr. Mukwege was once the only doctor at Panzi Hospital able to perform fistula surgery; now he has trained four others. The hospital does one thousand such operations a year.

Because of the prevalence of fistulas, the Panzi complex is soaked in urine. A fistula is a hole in the tissue between the woman's vaginal wall and bladder. A hole made by rape or shoving an instrument inside her vagina. A hole in her body. A hole in her soul. A hole where her confidence, her esteem, her spirit, her light, her urine leak out.

The smell pervades everything. Pee spills out of women in a huge, dirt-floored hangarlike space where hundreds sit all day. Pee spills out in classrooms, leaving puddles on the floor. The women are always wet. Their legs chafe and their skin burns. There are many little girls in pee-stained dresses roaming around Panzi; shy and ashamed, they, too, are victims of rape. The week of my visit, a state agency had turned off the water for the hospital after billing Panzi seventy thousand dollars (an insane amount by Congolese standards) because it heard that the hospital, which is private, was receiving money from the West. Staff had to bring in buckets of water from the surrounding neighborhood. To have hundreds of women with fistula-caused incontinence and no water seemed like a crime upon a crime.

I can't help wondering what happened in Dr. Mukwege's life that compelled him to work here, sometimes fourteen hours a day. "I was born in Bukavu on March 1, 1955," he tells me. "During my young age my mother was suffering with asthma. In the night when she became ill, I was the one who would go and look for a nurse or bring her medication. We all thought she would die. Even now, each birthday she celebrates, I am so happy to see her alive.

"My father was a pastor. He was very gentle, very human. From him I got the caring to treat patients. When we would go and visit sick people together, he would pray. I would ask, 'Why can't you give them tablets or prescriptions?' He said, 'I am not a doctor.' I decided then that prayer is not enough. People must take things into their own hands. Asking God does not change anything. He gives us the ability to say yes or no. You must use your hands, your mind. When I receive women here who are hungry, I can't say, 'God bless you.' I have to give them something to eat. When someone is suffering, I can't tell her about God, I have to treat her pain. You can't hide yourself in religion. Not a solution."

Dr. Mukwege began as a general practitioner, focusing on pediatrics. When he worked in a clinic in Lemera, a village south of Bukavu, he saw dreadful things happening in maternity. "Women were coming in bleeding day after day, many with severe infections. A woman had a baby and carried it dead in her vagina for a week. It was terrible. This helped me make a total engagement in a new career."

He went back to school to study gynecology in Angers, France, and then returned to Lemera to train the staff in obstetrics and gynecology. After he moved to Bukavu, he created a special maternity ward at Panzi. Women who were victims of extreme sexual violence began to arrive. The number grew every day.

Who was—and is—raping the women? The better question might be, who isn't?

The perpetrators include the Interahamwe, the Hutu fighters who fled neighboring Rwanda in 1994 after committing genocide there; the Congolese army; a loose assortment of armed civilians; even UN peacekeepers. Christine Schuler Deschryver, who cofounded the City of Joy with Dr. Mukwege and me (a sanctuary for survivors and a revolutionary center for leadership) and has been its director for nine years, a fierce advocate for Panzi Hospital and Congolese women, says, "All of them are raping women. It is a country sport. Any person in uniform is an enemy to women. This is an economic war. If you look at the map you will see that every place where there are mass rapes there is a coltan mine. Coltan is used for computers, PlayStations, and phones. Women are being raped and murdered so the world can have their phones."

Many women do not even report the violations, because they are afraid of rejection by their husbands and families. Although there are laws against rape in the Congo, if a woman reports her rape and her rapist is arrested, he can pay his way out and come back and rape her again. Or murder her.

Dr. Mukwege, in contrast, is motivating a different kind of healing army. I speak with a hospital employee named Bonane. "I was in Uganda," he says. "I saw the doctor on TV. He was explaining the atrocities. I realized these are my mothers and sisters. I was so inspired. I came here to work with him."

Dr. Mukwege is married with five children, but his brother, Herman, tells me his family doesn't see him much because his devotion to the women has consumed his life. Although the doctor's energy never flags, I notice an underlying exhaustion in his face and his being, a sleepless despair that comes from dwelling constantly amid violence and cruelty. He says to me, "When you rape a woman, you destroy life and you destroy your own life. Animals don't do this. When a pigeon has sex with another pigeon, it is kind. I am wondering how man has the power of such destruction."

And yet, the status of women in the Congo was dismal long before the wars started. The women work all day in the field and market, carrying the Congo on their backs (sometimes up to two hundred pounds in bags strapped to their foreheads). They prepare the dinner, wash the clothes, clean the house, take care of the children, have mandatory sex with their husbands. They have no power, no rights, and no value. Many women I talk to ask why I am "wasting my time" with them.

I interview a man who is the keeper of a gorilla preserve. He tells me that when dangerous militias began staking out territory in the park, he went to their commanders and asked if their soldiers would work with him to protect the gorillas. In the end they all agreed. I ask him why he didn't feel compelled to do the same for the women. The question surprised him. He had no answer.

I ask the doctor about the Congo's leader, Joseph Kabila, who in November 2006 became the country's first democratically elected president in forty-six years and promised to be the "craftsman of peace." Are things getting better?

Dr. Mukwege sighs. "Kabila," he says, "has done nothing. The fighting here in the east has not stopped. During 2004 my life was threatened; I got phone calls warning me to stop my work or die. The calls have ceased, but it is still very dangerous. (Since then there was one attempt on Dr. Mukwege's life, and he is constantly under threat. So much so that he is surrounded by UN guards and unable to leave the hospital grounds where he now lives as well.)

"Visitors come from the international community," he continues. "They eat sandwiches and cry, but they do not come back with help. Even President Kabila has never put his foot here. His wife was here. She wept, but she has done nothing."

Dr. Mukwege would at least like to get real protection for the women once they leave the hospital. "I patch them up and send them back home," he says, "but there is no guarantee they will not be raped again. There have been several cases where women have come back a second time, more destroyed than the first."

On my last day, the doctor asks me if I will lead some exercises for the women that will help alleviate their trauma. We go to the hangarlike building where 250 traumatized and sick women are waiting. We begin with breathing. Inhale, exhale. Inhale, exhale. Then we attach a noise to the breath. Other noises follow. One after another, noise after noise. Then we attach a movement. There is stomping. There is punching. There is mad waving of arms. The women are up on their feet, screaming, releasing guttural sounds of sorrow, rage, and terror.

In the midst of this energy, Dr. Mukwege challenges the women to a dance contest. Celebration and power explode from their bodies. A part of each woman is fierce, unbreakable. No one has killed their spirits. The doctor whispers to me, "When I see this joy, this life in the women, I know why I must come back here every day."

The women's frenzy builds and builds. They dance in the hot African sun. They dance in the open road. They literally dance us up a steep hill, hundreds of women and children moving in a single, radiant feminine mass.

If 250 women who have been raped, torn, starved, and tortured can find the strength to dance us up a mountain, surely the rest of us can find the resources and will to guarantee their future.

Baptized

BUKAVU, DEMOCRATIC REPUBLIC OF THE CONGO, 2007

Look out your window
The dead live everywhere
Think of your luxuries, your cell phones
as corpses
I held an eight-year-old girl in my lap
Who had been raped by so many men
She had an extra hole inside her
When she accidentally peed on me
I was baptized
It isn't over there
The Congo
It's inside everything you touch and do
Or do not do.

The Bureau of Sex Slavery

PARIS, 2015

I wrote this monologue for La Domenica di Repubblica *on the occasion of November 25, the International Day for the Elimination of Violence against Women. It was republished in* Le Monde *and the* Nation.

I am thinking of the price list leaked out from the ISIS Sex Slave Market, which included women and girls on the same list as cattle. ISIS needed to impose price controls as they were worried about a downturn in their market.

Women ages forty to fifty were priced at $40; women thirty to forty, at $69; women twenty to thirty, $86; and girls one to nine, $172. Women over fifty weren't even listed. They had no market value. They were discarded like milk cartons with expired sale dates. But they weren't simply abandoned in some smelly dung heap of trash. First, they were probably tortured, beheaded, raped, and then thrown into a pile of rotting corpses. I am thinking of a one-year-old child's body for sale and what it would be like for a hefty, sex-deprived, war-driven thirty-year-old soldier to buy her, package her, take her home like a new television. What would he be feeling or thinking as he unwrapped her baby flesh and raped her with his penis the size of her tiny body?

I am thinking that in 2015 I am actually reading an online Best Practices for Sex Slavery manual with step-by-step instructions and rules of how to treat your sex slave published by a very organized wing of a rogue government (Bureau of Sex Slavery) with the unapologetic mandate of regulating the raping, beating, buying, and enslaving of women.

Here are examples of the dos and don'ts in the manual: "It is permissible to beat the female slave as a [form of] *darb ta'deeb* [disciplinary beating], [but] it is forbidden to [use] *darb al-takseer* [literally, breaking beating], [*darb*] *al-tashaffi* [beating for the purpose of achieving gratification], or [*darb*] al-*ta'dheeb* [torture beating]. Further, it is forbidden to hit the face."

I am wondering how the ISIS bureaucrats will distinguish punches, kicks, and choking as acts of discipline from acts of sexual gratification. Will a team from the bureau break in and check for hard-ons as the beatings of slaves occur? And how will they know what actually made the soldier hard? Many men get turned on solely by the assertion of power. And if it is determined that the soldier beat or choked or kicked his slave for pleasure, what will the punishment be? Will the soldier be forced to return the slave and lose his deposit, pay a steep fine, or simply be made to pray harder?

I am thinking how easy it is to make ISIS a monstrous aberration when they are in fact an outcome of a long continuum of multiple crimes and disorders. Their sexual atrocities only vary in design and application from many other warlords in other wars. What's shocking and new is the brazen and unabashed display of these advertised crimes on the internet, the commercial normalization of these atrocities, the ISIS apps, using sex as a recruiting tool. Their work and its rapid proliferation don't exist in a historical vacuum.

It is escalated and legitimized by centuries of rampant impunity for sexual violence. This led me to thinking about the comfort women, the first modern-day sex slaves. These young girls from Asia were abducted in their prime by the Japanese Imperial Army in World War II to be held in Comfort stations, providing sex to Japanese soldiers in service of their country. The women were raped sometimes seventy times a day. If they got too tired and were unable to move, they would chain them to their beds and continue raping them like limp sacks. The comfort women were silenced in their shame for forty-five years and then for twenty-five years since they have marched and stood vigil in the rain demanding justice. And now, only a few remain, while only last month the Japanese prime minister Shinzo Abe sidestepped a direct apology yet again. This inertia, silence, paralysis has stalled and prevented investigation and prosecution into sexual crimes against Muslim, Croat, and Serb women raped in camps in the former Yugoslavia; Black women and girls raped on plantations in the South; Jewish women and girls raped in German concentration camps; Indigenous women and girls raped on reservations in the United States.

I am hearing the cries of the permanently unsettled ghosts of violated women and girls in Bangladesh, Sri Lanka, Haiti, Guatemala, Philippines, Sudan, Chechnya, Nigeria, Colombia, Nepal, the list goes on. I am thinking of the last eight years I spent in the Democratic Republic of the Congo, where a similar conflagration of predatory capitalism, centuries of colonialism, endless war, and violence in the name of mineral theft has left thousands of women and girls without organs, sanity, families, or a future. And how terms like re-raped have now become re re re re raped.

I've been writing this same piece for twenty years. I have tried it with data and detachment, passion and pleading, existential despair, and how even now as I write I wonder if we have evolved a language to meet this century that would trump a piercing wail.

Every patriarchal institution has failed to intervene in any meaningful way, and structures like the United Nations amplify the problem, as peacekeepers, meant to protect the women and girls, are rapists themselves.

I am thinking of Shock and Awe and how it helped unleash Rape and Behead. We all knew then in our bodies and beings as we marched against the pointless immoral war on Iraq, millions of us disregarded citizens around the world, what shrapnel-filled hurts and humiliations and darkness would be torn asunder with those deadly three thousand U.S. Tomahawk missiles.

I am thinking of religious fundamentalism and God the Father and how many women have been raped in his name and how many massacred and murdered. I am thinking about the notion of rape as prayer, rape as prayer, rape as prayer, and a Theology of Rape, a religion of Rape. And how this practice is one of the largest world religions, growing hundreds of converts every day as—according to the United Nations—one billion women will be beaten or raped in their lifetime.

I am thinking of the manic speed at which new and grotesque methods for commodifying and desecrating the bodies of women multiply in a system where what is most alive, whether the earth or women, must be objectified and annihilated in order to escalate consumption and "growth."

I am thinking of the thousands of young men and women from the West between the ages of fifteen and twenty who signed up to join ISIS. What were they looking for, what were they running from? Poverty, alienation, Islamophobia, a desire for meaning and purpose? Belonging?

I am thinking or maybe I am unable to think, caught inside the ongoing mindfuck of this century. Knowing on the one hand the only way forward is a total rewriting of the current story, a deep and studied collective examination of root causes of the various violences in all their economic, psychological, racial, patriarchal parts, which requires time, and at the same moment knowing that here and now three thousand Yazidi women are being beaten, raped, and tortured.

I am thinking of the women, the thousands of women around this world who have worked endlessly for years and years exhausting every fiber of their beings to make rape real, to end this pathology of violence and hatred toward us and no matter how logical we are, how patient, how empathetic, how many studies we do, how many numbers we show, how many survivors we treat, how many stories we hear, how many daughters we bury, how many cancers we get, the war against us rages on, each day more methodical, more brazen, brutal, more psychotic. ISIS, like rising sea levels, melting glaciers, and murderous temperatures, may be the scalding indicator that the endgame for women is near. The day has arrived when eons of women's rage must in turn coalesce into a fiery volcanic force unleashing the global vagina fury of female goddesses Kali, Oya, Pele, Mama Wati, Hera, Durga, Inanna, and Ixchel and let our wrath lead the way.

I am thinking of the famous female Yazidi folk singer, Xate Shingali, who, after finding the heads of her sisters hanging from poles in her village square, asked the Kurdish government to arm and train the women, and how now the Sun Girls, the women's militia she formed, are fighting ISIS in the mountains of Sinjar. And in this moment, after years of working to end violence, I am dreaming of thousands of crates of AK-47s, falling from the skies, landing in the villages and centers and farms and lands of women, breasted warriors rising in armies for life.

This led me to love, thinking about love, how the failure of this century is a failure of love. What are we being called to do, what are we really made of, each of us alive on this planet today? What kind of love, what depth of love, what fierceness and searing love is required? Not a naive sentimental neoliberal love, but an unrelenting selfless love. A love that would vanquish systems built on the exploitation of multitudes for the benefit of the few. A love that would catalyze our numb revulsion at crimes against women and humanity into unstoppable collective resistance. A love that revered mystery and dissolved hierarchy. A love that found value in our connection rather than in our competing. A love that ensured we opened our arms to fleeing refugees rather than building walls to keep them out or teargassing them or removing their dead bloated bodies from our beaches. A love that would burn so bright it would permeate our deadness and melt our walls, ignite our imaginations, and inspire us to finally break out of this story of death.

Disaster Patriarchy

I wrote this piece for the Guardian's *two-hundredth-year celebration.*

COVID has unleashed the most severe setback to women's liberation in my lifetime. While watching this happen, I have started to think we are witnessing an outbreak of disaster patriarchy.

Naomi Klein was the first to identify "disaster capitalism." This is when capitalists use a disaster to impose measures they couldn't possibly get away with in normal times, generating more profit for themselves. Disaster patriarchy is a parallel and complementary process, where men exploit a crisis to reassert control and dominance, and rapidly erase hard-earned women's rights. All over the world, patriarchy has taken full advantage of the virus to reclaim power—on the one hand, escalating the danger and violence to women, and on the other, stepping in as their supposed controller and protector. (The term *racialized disaster patriarchy* was first used by Rachel E. Luft in writing about an intersectional model for understanding disaster ten years after Hurricane Katrina.)

I have spent months interviewing activists and grassroots leaders around the world, from Kenya to France to India, to find out how this process is affecting them, and how they are fighting back. In very different contexts, five key factors come up again and again. In disaster patriarchy, women lose their safety, their economic power, their autonomy, their education, and they are pushed onto the frontlines, unprotected, to be sacrificed.

Part of me hesitates to use the word *patriarchy*, because some people feel confused by it, and others feel that it's archaic. I have tried to imagine a newer, more contemporary phrase for it, but I have watched how we keep changing language, updating and modernizing our descriptions in an attempt to meet the horror of the moment. I think, for example, of all the names we have given to the act of women being beaten by their partner. First, it was battery, then domestic violence, then intimate partner violence, and most recently intimate terrorism. We are forever doing the painstaking work of refining and illuminating, rather than insisting the patriarchs work harder to deepen their understanding of a system that is eviscerating the planet. So, I'm sticking with the word.

In this devastating time of COVID we have seen an explosion of violence toward women. Intimate terrorism in lockdown has turned the home into a kind of torture chamber for millions of women. We have seen the spread of revenge porn as lockdown has pushed the world online; such digital sexual abuse is now central to domestic violence, as intimate partners threaten to share sexually explicit images without victims' consent.

The conditions of lockdown — confinement, economic insecurity, fear of illness, excess of alcohol — were a perfect storm for abuse. It is hard to determine what is more disturbing: the fact that in 2021 thousands of men still feel willing and entitled to control, torture, and beat their wives, girlfriends, and children, or that no government appears to have thought about this in planning for lockdown.

In Peru, hundreds of women and girls have gone missing since lockdown was imposed, and are feared dead. According to official figures reported by Al Jazeera, 606 girls and 309 women went missing between March 16 and June 30 2020. Worldwide, the closure of schools has increased the likelihood of various forms of violence. The Rape, Abuse and Incest National Network in the United States says its helpline for survivors of sexual assault has never been in such demand in its twenty-six-year history, as children are locked in with abusers with no ability to alert their teachers or friends. In Italy, calls to the national antiviolence toll-free number increased by 73 percent between March 1 and April 16, 2020, according to the activist Luisa Rizzitelli. In Mexico, emergency call handlers received the highest number of calls in the country's history, and the number of women who sought domestic violence shelters quadrupled.

To add outrage to outrage, many governments reduced funding for these shelters at the exact moment they were most needed. This seems to be true throughout Europe. In the U.K., providers told Human Rights Watch that the COVID-19 crisis has exacerbated a lack of access to services for migrant and Black, Asian and minority ethnic women. The organizations working with these communities say that persistent inequality leads to additional difficulties in accessing services such as education, health care, and disaster relief remotely.

In the United States, more than five million women's jobs

were lost between the start of the pandemic and November 2020. Because much of women's work requires physical contact with the public — restaurants, stores, childcare, health-care settings — theirs were some of the first to go. Those who were able to keep their jobs were often frontline workers whose positions have put them in great danger; some 77 percent of hospital workers and 74 percent of school staff are women. Even then, the lack of childcare options left many women unable to return to their jobs. Having children does not have this effect for heterosexual fathers. The rate of unemployment for Black and Latina women was higher before the virus, and now it is even worse.

The situation is more severe for women in other parts of the world. Shabnam Hashmi, a leading women's activist from India, tells me that by April 2020 a staggering 39.5 percent of women there had lost their jobs. "Work from home is very taxing on women as their personal space has disappeared, and workload increased threefold," Hashmi says. In Italy, existing inequalities have been amplified by the health emergency. Rizzitelli points out that women already face lower employment, poorer salaries, and more precarious contracts, and are rarely employed in "safe" corporate roles; they have been the first to suffer the effects of the crisis. "Pre-existing economic, social, racial and gender inequalities have been accentuated, and all of this risks having longer-term consequences than the virus itself," Rizzitelli says.

When women are put under greater financial pressure, their rights rapidly erode. With the economic crisis created by COVID, sex- and labor-trafficking are again on the rise. Young women who struggle to pay their rent are being preyed on by landlords, in a process known as "sextortion."

I don't think we can overstate the level of exhaustion, anxiety, and fear that women are suffering from taking care of families, with no break or time for themselves. It's a subtle form of madness. As women take care of the sick, the needy, and the dying, who takes care of them? Colani Hlatjwako, an activist leader from the Kingdom of Eswatini, sums it up: "Social norms that put a heavy caregiving burden on women and girls remain likely to make their physical and mental health suffer." These structures also impede access to education, damage livelihoods, and strip away sources of support.

UNESCO estimates that upward of eleven million girls may not return to school once the COVID pandemic subsides. The Malala Fund estimates an even bigger number: twenty million. Phumzile Mlambo-Ngcuka, from UN Women, says her organization has been fighting for girls' education since the Beijing UN women's summit in 1995. "Girls make up the majority of the schoolchildren who are not going back," she says. "We had been making progress—not perfect, but we were keeping them at school for longer. And now, to have these girls just dropping out in one year, is quite devastating."

Of all these setbacks, this will be the most significant. When girls are educated, they know their rights, and what to demand. They have the possibility of getting jobs and taking care of their families. When they can't access education, they become a financial strain to their families and are often forced into early marriages.

This has particular implications for female genital mutilation (FGM). Often, fathers will accept not subjecting their daughters to this process because their daughters can become breadwinners through being educated. If there is no education, then the traditional practices resume, so that daughters can be sold for dowries. As Agnes Pareiyo, chairwoman of the Anti–Female

Genital Mutilation Board in Kenya, tells me: "COVID closed our schools and brought our girls back home. No one knew what was going on in the houses. We know that if you educate a girl, FGM will not happen. And now, sadly the reverse is true."

In the early months of the pandemic, I had a front-row seat to the situation of nurses in the United States, most of whom are women. I worked with National Nurses United, the biggest and most radical nurses' union, and interviewed many nurses working on the front line. I watched as for months they worked grueling twelve-hour shifts filled with agonizing choices and trauma, acting as midwives to death. On their short lunch breaks, they had to protest over their own lack of personal protective equipment (PPE), which put them in even greater danger. In the same way that no one thought what it would mean to lock women and children in houses with abusers, no one thought what it would be like to send nurses into an extremely contagious pandemic without proper PPE. In some U.S. hospitals, nurses were wearing garbage bags instead of gowns and reusing single-use masks many times. They were being forced to stay on the job even if they had fevers.

The treatment of nurses who were risking their lives to save ours was a shocking kind of violence and disrespect. But there are many other areas of work where women have been left unprotected, from the warehouse workers who are packing and shipping our goods to women who work in poultry and meat plants who are crammed together in dangerous proximity and forced to stay on the job even when they are sick. One of the more stunning developments has been with "tipped" restaurant workers in the United States, already allowed to be paid the shockingly low wage of $2.13 an hour, which has remained the same for the past twenty-two years. Not only has work declined, tips have also declined greatly for those women, and now a new degradation called "maskular harassment" has emerged, where male customers insist waitresses take off their masks so they can determine if and how much to tip them based on their looks.

Women farmworkers in the United States have seen their protections diminished while no one was looking. Mily Treviño-Sauceda, executive director of Alianza Nacional de Campesinas, tells me how pressures have increased on *campesinas,* or female farmworkers: "There have been more incidents of pesticide poisonings, sexual abuse and heat stress issues, and there is less monitoring from governmental agencies or law enforcement due to COVID-19."

COVID has revealed the fact that we live with two incompatible ideas when it comes to women. The first is that women are essential to every aspect of life and our survival as a species. The second is that women can easily be violated, sacrificed, and erased. This is the duality that patriarchy has slashed into the fabric of existence, and that COVID has laid bare. If we are to continue as a species, this contradiction needs to be healed and made whole.

To be clear, the problem is not the lockdowns but what the lockdowns, and the pandemic that required them, have made clear. COVID has revealed that patriarchy is alive and well; that it will reassert itself in times of crisis because it has never been truly deconstructed; and that, like an untreated virus, it will return with a vengeance when the conditions are ripe.

The truth is that unless the culture changes, unless patriarchy is dismantled, we will forever be spinning our wheels. Coming out of COVID, we need to be bold, daring, outrageous and to imagine a more radical way of existing on the earth. We need to continue to build and spread activist movements. We need progressive grassroots cisgender, transgender, and nonbinary people of color in positions of power. We need a global initiative on the scale of a Marshall Plan or larger, to deconstruct and exorcise patriarchy—which is the root of so many other forms of oppression, from imperialism to racism, from transphobia to the denigration of the earth.

There would first be a public acknowledgment, and education, about the nature of patriarchy and an understanding that it is driving us to our end. There would be ongoing education, public forums and processes, studying how patriarchy leads to various forms of oppression. Art would help expunge trauma, grief, aggression, sorrow, and anger in the culture and help heal and make people whole. We would understand that a culture that has intentional amnesia and refuses to address its past can only repeat its misfortunes and abuses. Community and religious centers would help members deal with trauma. We would study the high arts of listening and empathy. Reparations and apologies would be done in public forums and in private meetings. Learning the art of apology would be as important as prayer.

The feminist author Gerda Lerner wrote in 1986: "The system of patriarchy in a historic construct has a beginning and it will have an end. Its time seems to have nearly run its course. It no longer serves the needs of men and women, and its intractable linkage to militarism, hierarchy and racism has threatened the very existence of life on Earth."

As powerful as patriarchy is, it's just a story. As the post-pandemic era unfolds, can we imagine another system, one that is not based on hierarchy, violence, domination, colonialization, and occupation? Do we see the connection between the devaluing, harming, and oppressing of women and the destruction of the earth itself? What if we lived as if we were kin? What if we treated each person as sacred and essential to the unfolding story of humanity?

What if rather than exploiting, dominating, and hurting women and girls during a crisis, we designed a world that valued them, educated them, paid them, listened to them, cared for them, and centered them?

Freeing the Birdsong

FEBRUARY 2022

In February 2022, I curated a series in the Guardian *called "Living in a Woman's Body." I asked a group of cisgender and transgender women and gender-diverse people to write the story their body needed to tell. The series was meant to complement and inspire women in One Billion Rising, a global protest campaign to end rape and all forms of violence against women and gender-diverse people, who in 2022 were Rising for the Bodies of All Women, Girls, and the Earth.*

For so many years I lived as if I didn't have a body. Mine was a conquered land, a place that had been pillaged and vanquished from the very start.

Thirteen years ago, I found out I had stage 3/4 uterine cancer. I discovered it late. By the time I did, a tumor the size of an avocado had already grown and occupied my uterus. It had busted through my colon. I did not know it or feel it. I did not live in my body.

I traveled the world in search of answers, asking women everywhere: When did you leave your body? Who owns your body? What space is your body allowed to occupy? How has your body been hurt changed or refused by these forces—the government, your job, the Supreme Court, white supremacy, climate catastrophe, poverty, police violence, settler colonialism, transphobia, imperialism, capitalism? When does your body rest? How does your body fight back? What is the story your body needs to tell? What is a body? What were you taught to believe about your body? Can you hear the body of the earth? What is she saying?

Women's bodies are forever under threat. On alert. Ducking. Crouching. Hiding. Making themselves smaller. Less obvious or outrageously obvious. Waiting for the insult. Guarding against the unwanted touch. The grab. The punch. The rape. The murder.

Nurses expected to sacrifice their bodies for those who refuse to wear masks and protect their own bodies. Women restaurant workers forced to take down their masks, to risk sickness and death, so the unmasked customer can decide if their face is pretty enough for his lousy tip. Women farmer's bodies assaulted while harvesting the fields. They call them the *field de calzon*— the field of panties because their panties are ripped off them when they are raped.

Black women's bodies shot by police in their beds, in their cars, hallways, shot for a traffic violation in front of their child, killed on a wellness check, the wrong body in the wrong house. Bodies needing care, needing rest, killed for simply being there. Then after, even their stories and names are disappeared. Speak her body, say her name.

Body of girl child sold by her parents to an old man in Herat, Afghanistan, to keep her starving family alive, sold online for the price of a cell phone. Other underaged girls sourced by a British socialite for her rich sadistic boyfriend who serves the girl child's body to his luminous circle of the depraved.

Women's bodies carrying the memories of trauma in the form of cysts, tumors, bumps, and lumps that grow where the meanness left its mark.

Women's bodies always serving, feeding, bathing, holding, carrying, nurturing other bodies, bodies who never have time to think about their own.

Women's bodies hated for their "perfection," for their "imperfection," hated for being too thin, too fat, too round, too flat. Hated because they can do all that and make you feel all that.

Bodies remembering, reattaching, returning, becoming body for the first time, becoming whole rested bodies. The burning from unwanted daddy fingers shoved inside at five, now becoming word, becoming fire, the language of purpose, of power.

Bare-breasted bodies in the streets pushing back against femicide. Indigenous women's bodies on horseback, in kayaks on the river standing off pipelines about to spill oil. Fist-raised bodies pressed right up against rows of erupting police. Hundreds of differently abled bodies occupying the corridors of Congress.

Enraged bodies smashing the steel doors of a factory where their
fellow workers needlessly died. Women's bodies unapologeti-
cally alive, freeing the beauty and birdsong inside, no longer
captive or denied, becoming one, surging body, sweeping in the
other ready bodies as they rise.

V

GRIEF

Perhaps the story we are afraid to tell is that we humans are made as much of grief as we are of stars. Our bodies, more river than bone, grown inside that sacred sac of nutrients and sorrow. What is the heart, but a core deposit of crude emotion passed from one generation to the next?

For much of my life, I have traveled this river taken by unyielding currents, bloodied by inexorable rocks. It called me early on. Not because I was brave but because I was bleeding. I hungered to know the wound. Or rather I hungered to swim through that portal to the other side.

Folding

They were lined up, your things like body bags, like stranded organs. I fold the blue-and-white-striped cotton shirt. It is soft and I remember you were carrying me in your arms and our baby was dying and the way the light and the soft white and blue made your tanned face look so fragile. I remember you once wore that shirt to the beach 'cause you were sunburned. The way you put on the thick white cream but never rubbed it in properly so that people would feel sorry for you, as it made you look sick or deranged. Hard to tell. And I remember you wearing the white-and-blue-striped shirt with maybe sneakers and there was this spring air and I met you for iced cappuccinos and we smoked too many cigarettes. We were celebrating an opening, I think. I believed you when you said you lived for the sound of my typewriter.

I fold the shirt and my hands are sweating like you used to sweat when you would chew too much gum after quitting drinking and you would get severe stomach cramps. Bent over in an airport terminal. Everything you did was extreme.

M, your chest was a monument. It was home plate. We went on for years. It was an accident. Love. You'd come back to bed after too much coffee and the front page, and we'd hold each other and start over. Your chest, a few perfectly placed straggly gray hairs. Your underarms soft. For a time, I dreamed of living there.

I'm folding this white-and-blue-striped shirt and there are boats we have been on and trains and airplanes. And motorcycle rides and dogs. Both of them rescued. Both of them bit people. And our cat, Simon we discovered was Simone ten years later, now rubbing the shirt. I remember the way we would spot each other in the distance and move toward each other, caught in that smile like we had just met. The way you loved pickles and hero sandwiches and liquids and anything chocolate and strange country music and playing dead and slicing my leather boots when you got angry and ripping the refrigerator door off, your fist made holes in the walls and we covered them with cheap prints of wild animals. I didn't give you enough. No one giving you enough. The nature of love and origins and holes too wide making more impossible holes.

Meat and potato man, alligator man. I'm folding your white-and-blue-striped shirt. Wish I could keep this smell. The sounds you made in your throat, always clearing your throat. Something always stuck there.

You promised we would grow old together. You promised you'd come back to save me, and you did, and we got better. No shakes anymore. No anxiety attack on the grocery line. We lived through Libya, Grenada, Carter, Bush, Reagan, Three Mile Island, AIDS, one million in Central Park against nuclear war, hostages, Abbie dying, Berlin Wall coming down, Tiananmen Square, Mandela free, acid rain.

I am folding this shirt, my hands trembling 'cause alone, I am alone. When these things go, when the body bags are removed, just the dried blood on the ground and the shadow outline like after a crime but this wasn't one. It was an accident. A momentous occasion that somehow went on for years and became something called my life.

I met you in a bar and you were handsome, sober, and hyper, and it was sweaty and summer in one-room apartments and we made love nine hours and lost afternoons, and this was the beginning of my adult life. I had never been with one person before, never said yes let's find out where this goes. Let's go the whole way and see and we stopped growing in the same direction.

I am going to be alone when these things go. Hold me. Don't stop, M. This was the great event. You, M.

I won't get to watch your hair turn white and you, grumpy and old and cantankerous. Hard to believe I wanted that, but I did. I fold the shirt and I keep trying to swallow. My throat closing like the trapdoor on the witch's castle in the Wizard of Oz. July comes and the people return, and it stays light longer and longer. You were as close to it as I've come, or I may ever come. The boats pulling out. The voices of the children painfully loud, screaming now in the late summer day.

Theresienstadt

1991

We arrived at Theresienstadt on October 15, 1991, for the commemoration of the fiftieth anniversary. The first transport arrived there in October 1941. I traveled to Czechoslovakia with my dear friend Michelle; her sister, Denise; and her mother, Helen, who was a survivor of the camp.

I

The leaves are falling on the way to Theresienstadt. The rain begins and the huge bus windshield wipers swat at the beginning drops and smash them like molecules that never got born. Michelle's teeth hurt. She holds her mouth. Michelle is going on a bus to a place where people starved and humiliated her mother. She was forced into a cramped cattle car with a thousand terrified people, and it was dark and smelly, and she could not see out. Michelle is going on a bus to a place that has possessed her dreams, haunted her imagination. It is a rancid place, a place that has lived in the pit of Michelle's stomach like a tumor, tearing if she moved too fast or spoke too loudly or desired too much. This is a place that murdered Michelle's grandparents, drowned them in typhus and dysentery and despair. Michelle is thirty-nine years old. She lives in a sunny place in California. She has a new son. She is going on a bus to a place that is surrounded by startling green trees and spacious roads, and there are little shops that sell small umbrellas with cartoon animals and happy townspeople drinking beer and eating salami.

Michelle's teeth ache more and more as the bus gets closer. She holds her mouth and pushes her teeth into her head as if the pressure would prevent an invisible wind from seizing them. Denise, Michelle's older sister, is on the bus too. Denise is forty-one years old. She lives near a fire station in a small town in New Jersey. She is comforted by the loud noise of the fire engines. She is comforted being near the danger because the danger is so familiar, and she is comforted by the idea of rescue. Nazis have been main characters in Denise's dreams since she was little. Denise paints pictures for children's books, fairy-tale images, dragons and unicorns and bunnies with wings. Michelle and Denise begin to talk rapidly as the bus gets closer to the place.

Michelle's mother, Helen is also on the bus. She is sixty-nine years old. Her face tightens as the bus passes piles of burning coal. She is going back after fifty years to a place that changed her spiritual chemistry, permanently erased her belief in God. She is going back to a place that publicly hung people in order to teach other people a lesson, a place where so many people died daily their bodies filled the streets and were removed by death carts and then taken to the crematorium. She is going back to a place where for three years she waited daily to be transported east where her friends were forced at gunpoint to enter small metal rooms where the door was locked, and gas came, and they clawed frantically and died. Helen is going back to a place where she grew beets and onions, where she dug and harvested vegetables for the Nazi SS and because she gardened, she somehow lived. She is going back to a place where she stood by her dying mother's bed and somehow had to summon the strength to tell her mother, when she called out for her husband, that he was already dead from dysentery.

Helen is going back to a place, but this time she has her two daughters with her. Michelle fears that her mother has been able to keep back the memories, but like a hurricane they could sweep over her at any moment and whisk her permanently out to sea. Denise is afraid she will become too emotional and will not be able to be strong for her mother. Helen is worried that Michelle is too sensitive, and the experience will disturb her too much. She tried to protect her daughters. She didn't want them to live in terror. It seems clear that what happened to Helen and millions of Jews during the Holocaust was too big to conceal. Denise and Michelle are careful and gentle and fragile and deeply kind. They are haunted by floating demons, by a history and a place they were never physically a part of. Now, they are on the bus, the three of them. They are going back to a place together, to be there, to witness.

II

At first Helen recognizes nothing. She does not remember trees being there at all. There were no trees she thinks, nothing green. She keeps turning and spinning hoping to land on the right spot that will lead her in a familiar direction. She is lost.

There are hundreds of other survivors from the place who have come back. They frantically stare at one another like they just woke up from something. They are a gallery of faces, chiseled and worried, broken yet shockingly alive. It rains. Helen speaks Czech to strangers, and Michelle and Denise firmly hold their umbrellas like flags, liberating an unseen army. It feels frozen at the place.

How did you survive, Helen?

"Chance."

We are led around Theresienstadt. It is bleak and gray and strangely beautiful. Every spot is a location of loss or terror or last-minute survival. We pass an overgrown field where everyone thinks Helen grew vegetables for the SS. We pass the place where Jews were hung to teach a lesson to other Jews. We pass the place where the cattle cars came to bring more Jews. We pass the crematorium and death carts.

Helen's parents died here of dysentery and typhoid. She felt grateful they were spared the gas chamber. Michelle's and Denise's sadness explodes thinking of their grandparents, of their mother witnessing and trying to explain, trying to comprehend her parents dead.

We pass barracks that were stockades for thousands of over-crowded Jews. Some slept without blankets on the cold cement floor. We pass Helen's room, empty, a hundred cots, and cold, Nazi clean. We pass graveyards, and ashes coat our tongues.

Helen's walk around Theresienstadt is not an escaping walk. It is a conquering walk as if each step overtakes a Holocaust moment, each space leaps over a historical abyss.

Helen's walk around Theresienstadt is her reentry. Part of her is an astronaut circling for the last fifty years in space having been shot out of the engines of cruelty and horror. Helen is stepping back into the frame of her life.

Helen's walk around Theresienstadt is the walk of an Olympic athlete. She gains momentum and energy and color. She gets funnier. Her appetite returns. She wants to talk, to tell everything.

This time Helen has witnesses, who make her experience real, witnesses who feel her pain. Michelle and Denise walk slowly. They absorb the details of their mother's past like crucial messages. They pause sometimes and they stare out. They weep. They climb inside their mother.

They realize mothers cannot protect us—not from Nazis, not from evil, not from death. They watch their mother release her torture—a flock of burning doves bursting out of a rainy winter German sky.

Where All the Grief

I used to wonder where all the grief
of all the people went.
I would stare at strangers in parks and restaurants,
inspecting their faces for cracks of sorrow.
The grief was everywhere but nowhere you could touch.
I felt it in my room at night,
not ghostly exactly
but thick and pressing in.
On my haunches I rocked myself to sleep
to shake off the suffocating apparition.
I felt it in the clinking ice cubes of my parents' cocktail hour.
I felt it in the sluggish walk of those who worked
for the rich.
I felt it in the way my perfect beautiful mother
could not be found.
I felt it in the manic boys
grabbing at my teenage tits.
I was terrified the grief was waiting

somewhere,
terrified it was gathering,
terrified it would return one day
and swallow us whole.

And maybe it has
or is.

What is the military but the saluted straightjacket of
our mourning?
What are drones, assault rifles, and bombs but steely weapons
aimed at our sadness or anyone or thing that resembles it?
What is pornography but a gaudy performance of
our deepest loss and longing?

Today I stood in front of the muddy river in my backyard
after days of rain.
I thought of every river I've ever met—
every ocean and lake.
I thought of the salty aqua Adriatic that has healed
bitterness and bites in July.

I thought of Juhu Beach in Chennai, the procession of women
    of every age in their glittering pink purple golden saris at
    sunset
and the ambling cows
(I never saw a cow on a beach before).
I thought of the rough nakedness of the Atlantic at the tip of
    Montauk in late September
and dunking my bald head,
the saltwater stinging and cleansing the nicks

where I shaved the hairs falling from the chemo.
I thought of the Red Sea in Sharma El-Sheikh
and how all of us sought refuge there
right after the bombing.
And how my sister from Somalia
told me then, always, when the militias come, run to the sea.
I thought of the first time I crossed Lake Kivu from Goma to
   Bukavu
in Congo and the soft blue waxen horizon seemed at odds with
   so many macheted bodies below.
And my tears were muddy humid tears
that linked me to a muddy river in the village
in Kosova where the children were playing among
the garbage and human skulls,
linked me to cartoon communities of kooky penguins
on the sandy banks of Cape Town,
linked me to belly dancers moving with
the rhythm of subtle waves on the narrow boat on the Nile,
linked me to the wild low tide in Matabungkay Philippines.
We waded way out in high reeds
so stoned at eight in the morning.
It was the first time I literally got lost in the horizon.
My muddy tears linked me to the Seine, which is sometimes
   brown, sometimes green or black depending on light, the
   Seine
which has coursed through my life the way it courses through
   Paris.
The Seine, which has given me two books
and my body
after cancer.
And just weeks ago rising unnaturally high

flooding the city,
linking me to the Flint River in Michigan
twenty-five thousand kids exposed to lead poisoning.
Some with scabies and rashes, some stopped growing.
Some got aggressive.
And the children dying in the Niger Delta before they reach the
    hospitals from the oil contaminated water
life expectancy now dropped from seventy to forty-five.
Oil, oil, oil, tears of oil,
the carelessness of BP spilling oil and exploding
oil in the Gulf of Mexico
oil drenched pelicans and fish
and how that contamination led
to the loss of jobs which didn't allow for grieving
but desperation
which led to women being beaten
and humiliated by their unemployed husbands.

I sat down by the river and I wept for the lead in the water,
and sodium fluoride, mercury, arsenic, dioxins, polychlorinated
    biphenyls, chlorine, perchlorate, and the oil.
I wept for every ocean I have ever met and haven't met.
I wept for dolphins trapped in huge plastic wrappers and
    albatrosses
on Midway Atoll filled with bottle caps and batteries mistaken
    for food.
I wept for the children who would never know what it means
    to run arms wide open into a voluptuous sea without worry,
who see water as predator and not a source.
I wept for our selfishness and stupidity.
I wept for all those who will not weep

and cannot weep and refuse to let their weeping
join them to the sea of weeping
the muddy river of grieving.

I wept for the sixteen-year-old girl who trusted the sea
more than her own mother.
She would lay her naked lean body
half in and half out of the water,
long brown hair
becoming sand, broken shells and stone.

And she would strongly whisper
almost chant:
make me clam, coral, weed
make me jellyfish, trumpet conch, and crab
make me salty blue
make me transparent
Make me wild.

VI

FALLING

My beloved friend Elizabeth Streb, a renowned action dancer, says: "Falling? Nothing else is that interesting—mostly because you cannot control it. Ever. Falling is the second after you can no longer make any decisions. The future is finally 'now.' Falling is all that movement is. Control or any idea of acquiring skill, has nothing to do with movement. Nothing."

I don't remember a time I wasn't falling. I remember falling before I remember standing. I was named Eve, after the first fallen woman. I was the carrier of the fall.

I fell from great heights at ten years old. Once adored by my father, I was literally thrown out of his garden. I fell from grace, fell out of the family. I fell into violence.

I spent my early years pushing the edge of gravity. It was not fearlessness so much as practice. Learning how to fall without breaking. I became a high diver, falling and somersaulting through air. I jumped off high cliffs. The freedom of falling, the mad aliveness of falling. The glorious danger.

Perhaps my writing all these years has simply been a record of falling: fallen places and people and walls, the fallout of wars and pandemics, falling in and out of love, falling empires, the unhoused, the imprisoned, the raped, the exiled who fall through the cracks, falling to pieces, falling short of my own insanely high expectations, the fear of falling on deaf ears.

2020. The world fell out of touch and time. One kind of falling fell into another. Intersectional falling. Black women and transwomen and men falling to bullets of police in the streets of America, bodies falling in millions to COVID-19, millions of birds falling from the burning skies. Knees on necks, ventilator tubes shoved down throats. "I can't breathe." The walls of denial collapsing like massive sheets of Arctic ice. Falling and flooding.

How do you live on the edge of what's over?

Is precarious the only country?
Is falling the new language?
Are you sure you have it?
Has it always been there?
Does it make you want to shop?
Or clean?
Or count the dead?
Do you notice how often microbe creeps into the conversation?
Do you know where you fit in the hierarchy of the disposable?
Would you change places?
Really?
Are preexisting conditions equal to systemic oppression?
How do you shelter in place without place?
Have you ashamedly caught yourself comforted by thinking that
it's mainly the old who
will die and then remembered you were old?

What does it mean to be a carrier?
Who will you become at a distance?
Is choosing sickness or hunger a choice?
Whom haven't you noticed before?
Are they currently keeping you alive?
Will you remember them after?
Is mutiny possible in quarantine?

After the fires

KINGSTON, NEW YORK, 2020

Thousands tumbled from the sky
like small sacks
splattering on the window shields of abandoned cars
on the scorching blacktop of forever highways
almost bone
from hunger and hypothermia
Some never made it off the ground
Swallows
Warblers
dazed with a kind of sad hopping
Most had flown too far in the wrong direction
to escape the smoke
two breaths at a time
the way birds breathe
the efficiency was catastrophic.
We're all escaping something now.
They put her into a coma
so she wouldn't be too terrified,

her face tied and taped to the ventilator.
Tell me
Tell me
who is breathing us now?

Dear Mother (Earth)

KINGSTON, NEW YORK, 2019

In 2018, I wrote a book, The Apology. *I had waited most of life for my father to apologize to me for sexually abusing and battering me as a child. Even after he was dead and gone for thirty-one years, I still waited. So, I decided to write the apology from him that I needed to hear. It was an excruciating and ultimately liberating experience. But after I was finished, I realized there was an apology I needed to make.*

It began with the article about the birds, the 2.9 billion missing North America birds, the 2.9 billion birds that disappeared and no one noticed. The sparrows, blackbirds, and swallows who didn't make it, who weren't ever born, who stopped flying or singing or making their most ingenious nests, who didn't perch or peck their gentle beaks into moist black earth. It began with the birds. Hadn't we even commented in June, Celeste and I, that they were hardly here? A kind of eerie quiet had descended. But later they came back. The swarms of barn swallows and the huge ravens landing on the gravel one by one. I know it was after hearing about the birds, that afternoon I crashed my bike. Suddenly falling, falling, unable to prevent the catastrophe ahead, unable to find the brakes or make them work, unable to stop the falling. I fell and spun and realized I had already been falling, that we have been falling, all of us, and crows and conifers and ice caps and expectations—falling and falling and I wanted to keep falling. I didn't want to be here to witness everything falling, missing, bleaching, burning, drying, disappearing, choking, never blooming. I didn't want to live without the birds or bees and sparkling flies that light the summer nights. I didn't want to live with hunger that turned us feral or desperation that gave us claws. I wanted to fall and fall into the deepest, darkest ground and be finally still and buried there.

But Mother, you had other plans. The bike landed in grass and dirt and bang, I was ten years old, fallen in the road, my knees scraped and bloody. And I realized that even then nature was something foreign and cruel, something that could and would hurt me because everything I had ever known or loved that was grand and powerful and beautiful became foreign and cruel and eventually hurt me. Even then I had already been exiled, or so I felt, forever cast out of the forest. I belonged with the broken, the contaminated, the dead.

Maybe it was the sharp pain in my knee and elbow, or the dirt embedded in my new jacket, maybe it was the shock or the realization that death was preferable to the thick tar of grief coagulated in my chest, or maybe it was just the lonely rattling of the spokes of the bicycle wheel still spinning without me. Whatever it was. It broke. It broke. I heard the howling.

Mother, I am the reason the birds are missing. I am the cause of salmon who cannot spawn and the butterflies unable to take their journey home. I am the coral reef bleached death white and the sea boiling with methane. I am the millions running from lands that have dried, forests that are burning, or islands drowned in water.

I didn't see you, Mother. You were nothing to me. My trauma smelted arrogance and ambition drove me to that cracking pulsing city. Chasing a dream, chasing the prize, the achievement that would finally prove I wasn't bad or stupid or nothing or wrong. Oh, my Mother, what contempt I had for you. What did you have to offer that would give me status in the marketplace of ideas and achieving? What could your bare trees offer but the staggering aloneness of winter or greenness I could not receive or bear. I reduced you to weather, an inconvenience, something that got in my way, dirty slush that ruined my overpriced city boots with salt. I refused your invitation, scorned your generosity, held suspicion for your love. I ignored all the ways we used and abused you. I pretended to believe the stories of the fathers who said you had to be tamed and controlled—that you were out to get us.

I press my bruised body down on your grassy belly, breathing me in and out. I have missed you, Mother. I have been away so long. I am sorry. I am so sorry. I am made of dirt and grit and stars and river, skin, bone, leaf, whiskers, and claws. I am a part of you, of this, nothing more or less. I am mycelium, petal pistil and stamen. I am branch and hive and trunk and stone. I am what has been here and what is coming. I am energy and I am dust. I am wave and I am wonder. I am an impulse and an order. I am perfumed peonies and the single parasol tree in the African savannah. I am lavender, dandelion, daisy, dahlia, cosmos, chrysanthemum, pansy, bleeding heart, and rose. I am all that has been named and unnamed, all that has been gathered and all that has been left alone. I am all your missing creatures, all the sweet birds never born. I am daughter. I am caretaker. I am fierce defender. I am griever. I am bandit. I am baby. I am supplicant. I am here now, Mother. I am yours. I am yours. I am yours.

Cicadas

KINGSTON, NEW YORK, 2020

Are we like cicadas?
Burrowed now under the earth
Learning the language of falling
Deep in fecund soil
Covered with wet leaves, shame
And the last hints of white snow
Is this restless twitching
Dreaming grieving remembering
Our homes, skin
And earth, skin too?
It certainly feels like we are very far under
Floating in our separate husks
Forced finally to learn to read the dark
In this radical underground
Where we suffocate and drown
Or our yearning compels us
To remake ourselves.
The cicadas cannot sting or bite
Their only defense is to emerge in the millions.

VII

SKIN

For much of my life I felt like the creature in the David Lynch film Eraserhead. *Translucent and overexposed, quivering on a bedroom dresser. I needed a soft white cloth to swaddle me or a mother who wanted me to feel held and safe. Skin. Something to contain and cover me.*

I remember I was about ten in the car with my mother. We were in a suburban parking lot, and for some reason she felt compelled to tell me about nymphomaniacs. She said they were women who couldn't get enough. "Enough of what?" I asked. But honestly, I already knew.

Here's How We Like It

Do not come at us. Visit. Nestle up. Ask with gentle fingers. Wait for an answer. See if we open. Pretend there's all the time in the world. Pretend we're on a faded white bench by the sea. Pretend you're not after anything. You like sitting. You like smelling. You like waiting. Offer us something soft, something sweet, white chocolate, a taste of strawberry jam.

Don't come at us. Don't do that paw thing. Don't have to have it. Don't erase us in getting to the thing. Don't make us a thing. Be awkward. We love awkward. Don't have mastered the situation. We're not problems. We do not want to be mastered. Don't know what you're doing. Be lost. Fumble. Make a mess. Ask questions.

Don't break us. Because then we become numb and you will never satisfy us and you will feel incompetent and you will get agitated and you will have to really have it in spite of protests or terror. You will break and enter and we will get even further apart.

Stop worrying about arriving. We're not shopping malls. We're openings, causes, mysteries. We're asking you to keep going.

And one last thing, don't fall asleep right when it's over. Not for a little while anyway. A lot begins for us right when you think it's over. Talking or crying is still it. It's just coming out of another part of our body.

Hold us okay? Hold us when you think it's over.

All Snap in My Jaw

When you lay your hand in the crack of my ass and we fall asleep I feel like we're out in the woods and the mud's cooling off the bee bites. I'm counting on another country. I'm trying to believe you're not going to fuck around. Your hair is quantum physics. I leap over what I don't trust. You said I had to be more gentle. I've been hurt and now I'm a turtle all snap in my jaw. When you lay your hand in the crack of my ass, it's the missing piece, covering the shame, reminding me of it. Your tenderness makes me liquid, makes me crawl quickly on the carpet, makes me hyper, makes me lonely and thirsty, makes me want to break it, in half, in other halves. Decapitate the tenderness. Then I won't ever have to know how violent it was before you. How hard.

When you lay your hand in the crack of my ass, I bite the eraser off the pencil, send it spitting into the boy's brown hair in the row in front of me. You sleep with your head on my shoulder, and I don't feel I'm enough to make you safe, to make anyone safe and you purr and drool a little there and I picture little baby trout in the puddle that forms on my shoulder and they're leaping, the trout, like particles, like acts of faith, like things just been born. Bite bite. You ask me to try to be more gentle. I was once, you know, before. When it was green, and my hair had just started, and the little spoon went in and out of my mouth. I lick you and there's heat, quantum heat. I lick you and I know if I don't survive this, I won't ever be human. Keep your tongue there longer. Look at him when he's inside you. Those are his hands. This is your . . . He's touching it. He's gently touching it and this strange stroking, this hardly tangible almost delicately but definitely buttering soothing striving feels like what they say is love.

The War Has Begun

NEW YORK CITY, 2003

We stopped everything
outside the black metal gate.
You kissed my mouth.
The fog had lifted
and we climbed the stairs
I was wet.
Saddam Hussein had just come out.
There were big holes in everything.
Big crater holes.
He was walking and smiling
and you couldn't figure out
how to take my belt off, the one
with the bear on it.
I helped you
decapitate the center
your lips silky
spreading with the rest of me.
Scud bombers

Stud bombers
I'm not a target
You're not accurate.
We're a landscape.
It's emotional.
The war has begun.

We're bombing Baghdad
We're eating Chinese food.
For hours they're dropping
out of the skies.
Your tongue licks gently
Grabbing clumps of your sweaty hair
I'm hot
not like a missile
not like oil burning
I'm hot
like sun on slippery summer grass
like a cave where fur gathers.
I'm hot George Bush
stuttering anecdotes
spit it out George
get it up George
Now you're a rock
finishing what you set out to do.
You don't leave me.
Your hands stay with me, searching
for a shiny thing in the wet leaves
Your hands press on me
I'm an explosion
not a twenty-megaton bomb

not a five-year-old's brain
bursting into chunky kindergarten pieces
I'm an explosion
a woman
a string about to be pulled
a perfumed load of resistance
a vagina of smells and stories
spilling out
into your encouraging fingers
onto the worn and flowery sheets
into the raw and waiting streets.

It Will All Go Like This

PARIS, 2010

I will be stretched out
Painfully clean white sheets
The women with the strong hands
will have just changed the bed
They will have moved me carefully,
lifting my bruised and bony legs
I will try not to focus on
how their lifting
reveals the little of me
that is left
how easy their fingers
scratch my bones
how light my body is like Styrofoam
instead I will be looking out the window
appearing distracted maybe or grumpy
Not worried. I will be too bony for worry
Too near the other side
They will think it's a memory maybe

Or a longing or maybe they won't be
Thinking about me at all
I will wish they were more connected to me
The women
maybe
But I will question that wish too
Suddenly sentimental
and really, I will be grateful for their disassociation
it frees me to think
how clean sheets even now
feel like the beginning of something
and I will feel emotional then realizing
I have used up my beginnings

You kissing me in Hyde Park
the wool of your black peacoat
rubbing my neck
there were ducks
our mouths kept opening and opening
early fall
the beginning of falling
the beginning of a betrayal
that would make him
the other
make him
vomit the turkey on Thanksgiving
the only meal I ever cooked
which made him feel like home and I had
destroyed home with my kissing in Hyde Park
or him when he was still the one
there next to me driving the car through

the flooding streets of the south
the palm trees swaying and thrashing to the point of breaking
him driving me back
to my mother
her face
Florida wrinkled
him leaving me but waiting waiting outside
by the sea
to catch me or rush in maybe or block the pain
of her disbelief or indifference
when I told her that her husband, my father
had put his hands on my five-year-old parts
him always there waiting, wanting to fix me
or catch me or teach me
but never receive me
we kept beginning
waiting to really begin
he once told me it didn't matter if it only happened
once
but he knew there would come that time that moment
when we would make love and
we would finally get lost
that time never came
and now it wouldn't
surprising how little it seemed to matter
as little as the women with the strong hands
rubbing my thin skin
now just a little too roughly with
the washcloth
now
how little those promises

looking out the window
the wind moving everything
the pink oleander
the pine
the wind the wind the wind
moving everything.

Sometimes It's So Can't Stop

This was initially written for an anthology published in 2011,
Sugar in My Bowl: Real Women Write About Real Sex, *curated*
by Erica Jong.

Take off shirt
    Undo belt
    Clumsy
    You do it
    No, I'll do it
    Undo bra
    One more hook
    Strip down
Sometimes it's all about
    Skin just skin
    Just the way skin
Oh God, sometimes it's like mouth on mouth
    Teeth
    Tongue
    Have to
Sometimes

You thought you were friends
And this current
Turns into one week
In a small hotel room in East Berlin.
Sometimes it's
About watching
Or being watched
Undressing in front of them
In front of the big window
Sometimes it's you putting a hand
On yourself
And them watching
And Rome watching them
Watching
Sometimes
It's a crowded boat filled
With cheering tourists
On the Adriatic
As you're both caught there
Naked humping in the sand
And you don't stop
Sometimes it's scuff marks on the off-yellow carpet
In the posh South Kensington apartment
Sometimes it's a dare
Forty-five floors up
Mouth on them
In a building that once existed
And they come by the time
Sometimes it's driving on the mad
Italian speedway at a thousand miles
Your face buried in his jeans

Sometimes it's a melting hot
    Summer day and you're passed out
    In the afternoon
    And you wake up with his rugged face
    Between your legs
Sometimes it's the twenty-nine-year-old lean boy
    From the village
    With the curly black hair
    Who comes to your summer house
    On the edge of the sea
    And kisses you and you know it's August
    And you're suddenly not fifty-four
Sometimes it's a song
    Or a joint
    Or too much chocolate
Sometimes it's only chocolate
    Or birthday cake at midnight
    Because one of you is married
Sometimes he just says in a proper English accent
    Do you mind if I put my penis inside you and it occurs
    to you
    you don't
Sometimes it's that window
    Wide open in Montauk
    And it's so bright you're
    Only wearing sunglasses
    Looking out
    As the wild Aussie takes you from behind
    Sweating and screaming out
And sometimes
    It just happens in Portugal

For the first time in seven years
You find each other
And you're not afraid
Sometimes it's the hysteria that comes
After he has been that deep inside you
And the crying is a way of coming
And sometimes
It's riding them like a bronco
Or humping her like you're about to get there
And sometimes it's the three of you in a hot tub
And you end up entangled not knowing
Whose hair whose mouth whose hand whose breast
And sometimes you dress up
And they take it off you
Sometimes it's hardness
It's softness
It's grabbing
It's refusing
Embarrassing
Sometimes it's "You're beautiful"
or
"God, your ass"
"Your skin"
And sometimes it's so insanely funny
It's ridiculous
But mainly it takes longer
It's all preparation
You lose track of who begins
Who's on top
Who got more
Who's inside who.

Who Will We Become Without Touch?

KINGSTON, NEW YORK, 2020

In 2020, during the height of COVID and lockdown, I curated a series for the Guardian *with the poet Mahogany L. Browne titled* Power of Touch.

I am afraid of what I will become without touch. Already the frayed edges are beginning to show. So much of my life, and the lives of so many women, is found through touch. We touch our babies, we hold them to our breasts and bellies, we wash our aging mothers' bodies and comb and braid our daughters' hair. We massage and we pet, and we soothe, and we tickle. We know how to express loss and grief with our shuddering bodies and tears, transform our rage into medicine with the simplest caress. We know how the body is filled with microaggressions and macro ones. We know how to loosen ourselves into grieving and tighten ourselves into rage. And many of us are practiced in that particular hug that shelters, that relieves, that confirms. Hugging is how we know we are here. How we feel each other's

existence and meaning and value and substance. How we trans-
mit our love, our empathy, our care.

I am sure that so much of what we women do—so much of
our so-called beauty routines—has as much to do with touch
as with appearance. I cannot wait to have my hair washed at
the hairdresser. There is one particular woman; I will call her
Nina. Her hands are delicious and confident and kind, equally
firm and gentle. When she digs her long, waltzing fingers into
my scalp, mixed with the warm soapy water, I know salvation.
The same with the woman who does my nails, the little hand
massages, her fingers pressing deep into the stress of my palm,
the flesh-to-flesh contact and energetic exchange. I need that.
We need that. Particularly those of us who live alone, who don't
live with partners or spouses. Particularly those of us most likely
to perish from the virus—the older ones. Touch is how we go on.

I think of hairdressers, manicurists, masseuses, nurses, care-
givers, nannies, yoga teachers, acupuncturists, physical thera-
pists. Who will they touch again and when?

The other night, the person I live with, Celeste, a magical
being, was playing and suddenly threw themself on top of me.
Their body was perfectly heavy, and it felt unbelievably good to
feel their human weight, muscle flesh pressing down on me. It
had nothing to do with sex, but everything to do with life, connection, and vitality. They smushed me good. The imprint has
lasted. These are desperate times.

We all know the significance of touch. We know babies who
experience physical contact show increased mental capabilities
in the first six months of life. Touch makes your brain grow. And
we know that those seriously deprived become aggressive and
develop behavioral problems. Touch is how we become part of
this human community.

So here we are in the middle of this pandemic, knowing our cough can potentially kill; our body could be a lethal weapon. How do we make sense of this? How do we live with this unbearable skin hunger?

Part of the agony of this crisis is that even in death we are denied the possibility of touching the body. By four o'clock each afternoon, I can feel the disintegration begin. After a day of disembodied voices, blurred and frozen faces, loud news. After a day of ever-increasing numbers of the invisible dead, the bodies piling up in unseen warehouses, the back of huge trucks and cold-storage rooms. After a day of aerial shots of mass graves, wooden coffins stacked like boxes of invisible pain. After a day of wanting to reach through the screen, the void, the isolation, to feel a heart beating, take someone's hand, breathe with another's breath, I can feel myself begin to disappear.

The body cannot and does not exist now. Not in life. Not in death. Thousands are disappearing without fanfare or acknowledgment, without family or ritual.

I want to make each body a person, each person real. I want to know their story and who they loved and what they were most proud of and where they first discovered beauty and what horizon they looked out on for most of their days. But death is moving so fast. You go to the hospital. You leave your loved ones. You don't return. No touch, no closure, no body. Nobody. Nothing. No longer here.

I think of Claude Rains in *The Invisible Man* unwrapping the bandages around his head only to reveal there is absolutely nothing there. Nothing. No flesh, no face. No person. Nothing. I was ten years old the first time I saw that movie. I remember vomiting and staying up the whole night in terror and being afraid of the dark after that. But it wasn't the dark I was afraid of, it was the disintegration of the body, becoming meaningless, becoming nothing.

I discovered early the best defense against this horrifying dissolution was touch, kissing, massive amounts of physical contact, otherwise known as sex. I salvaged the world through my hands, body, mouth, and skin. As a young woman, I needed to press my flesh against almost everything and everyone. Of course, misogynists interpreted this as promiscuous, loose. They called me a slut. But mine was an existential crisis. I needed touch. I needed physical connection. It saved me from unbearable loneliness. It allowed me to feel my impact on the world. It gave me pleasure and agency. It let me know that I existed, that I was here. It allowed me to fulfill my desire and heal the deepest physical wounds. It taught me trust might be possible and gave me undeniable moments of comfort.

A friend reported that a venture capitalist recently told her he saw a "touchless" future. I fear this is what the technocrats and AI people and fascists are dreaming of—a touchless future. The body has always been that lowly human thing that got in the way—messy desire and rage and passion and sex. I come from the land of the sixties. My consciousness was fashioned there in that ecstatic river of sex, drugs, and rock and roll. There I learned that the body is the loci of revolution and change. So here, now, where our bodies are locked behind masks and gloves and screens and filters, where will the center of our revolution lie?

I light a candle every night for those who have left the world that day. I imagine their faces. I sometimes am able to find their names. I touch the candle and feel the warmth of the flame on my body. I try to make them real. I allow myself to grieve their loss.

My act of resistance is simple. I will have a healthy respect and fear of the virus. I will maintain physical distancing for now. But I will not be afraid of your body.

I will not kill off my yearning to touch you. I will let it guide me. I will fantasize about it. I will write about it. I will draw it. I will remember us cuddling in January, mad dancing in the protest last July. I will feel the soft skin of your precious hand in mine. I will embrace you as you cry and cherish the wetness of your tears on my blouse. I will feel the fire of rage in my belly and the impossible sorrow in my throat. And I will learn over time how to translate this hunger for your body, for your burning skin, into the making of this most necessary new world.

RECKONING

Reckoning is the antidote to fascism.

Let Him Be Our Unifier

KINGSTON, NEW YORK, 2016

This was written for the Guardian *nine months before Donald Trump became president of the United States.*

Donald Trump is not a leader or a presidential candidate. He is an outcome, a viral manifestation of a serious malignant illness. He is the mirror of our emptiness, the emptying out that has been happening to our country for a very long time.

He is an outcome of a two-party system that has consistently ignored the needs and wishes of the majority of Americans for generations.

He is the manifestation of celebrity culture where those who have everything are worshipped for their shiny success, and in the world of celebrity that shininess is a stand-in for principles, substance, and moral values.

He is personality over planning, symbol over substance, insipidness over insightfulness.

He is the outcome of the rich being able to buy anything, including our democracy.

He is an outcome of centuries of underlying unaddressed, massively denied, and metastasized racism.

He is the hatred of the poor and the needy, the denigration of immigrants and those seeking refuge from the devastation of U.S. wars and imperialism.

He is the outcome of an insidious exceptionalism—the bedrock belief that American lives are more precious and valuable than any Others, those we stigmatize, bomb, torture, murder, control, invade and whose economies we trash, whose resources we devour, whose futures we steal.

He is the outcome of fear that masquerades as bullying.

He is the manifestation of patriarchy and the endlessly indoctrinated belief that only a father will save us even though the mainly men who have been determining reality for this country and the planet have led us to near ruin.

He is the outcome of high-tech fantasy, virtual disconnection, TV reality shows.

He is proof of the duplicity of corporate-sponsored media that claim "neutrality" while reaping profits from propping up racists, tyrants, fascists, haters, and those who would seek to destroy the country.

He is the outcome of an insanely violent culture, increasingly unkind, with more bullying that normalizes cruelty, industrializes punishment, and declares endless war on its own citizens.

He is the consolidation of a government that devotes huge portions of its budget to building an imperial military rather than feeding and educating its own people, that wreaks havoc on the world rather than fighting climate change, that promotes the pillaging of the earth rather than ending violence against the people who inhabit it, that forces working people to police the world rather than providing them with meaningful work.

He is the product of a country with the most number of armed citizens in the world, where the average of eighty-nine firearms for every one hundred people leads to more deaths at the hands of fellow countrymen every year than international terrorists have killed ever.

He is the outcome of a country where police consistently murder Black people with little to no repercussions, and millions are living in perpetual incarceration.

He is the outcome of corrupt, self-seeking, extremist politicians who ignore the Constitution and make it their business to refuse any meaningful legislation from getting passed.

He is the outcome of an insidious, selfish morality where getting what you want, making money at any expense is the credo, and how we behave, whom we hurt, or destroy, what earth we eviscerate is inconsequential.

He is the holographic representation of the failure of a country, our denial, our refusal to act and rise for one another and to take responsibility for what our government, corporations, military are doing across the world.

He is a symptom of what happens when collective consciousness has divided and subdivided so many times within this neoliberal psychosis that we no longer know how to make alliances, build coalitions, and have each other's backs or stand with one another when the going gets rough.

He is an outcome of a country with denial as thick as its amnesia. We come to honor and idolize war criminals and racists and sexists and corporates who have destroyed the lives of millions.

He is an outcome of years and years of each of us being taught to fend for ourselves, fight for our own share, step over those who we are told are slower or weaker but who may in fact be deeper, more moral, or more considered.

He is an outcome of a world divided between winners and losers.

He is an outcome of fatigue and privilege and disenchantment and hopelessness and exclusion.

He is an outcome of cynicism and an imposed belief that there is nothing we can really do to overcome this corporate neoliberal imperialist racist sexist homophobic earth-hating transphobic system.

The moment of America has arrived. This is our reckoning, our karma come to roost. It is way beyond the question of whom we vote for in the upcoming election.

It is a question of who we are. What is America? What kind of country do we want this to be? What values and principles do we hold and cherish?

What will we do and what lengths will we go to, what collective imagination will we employ, what mighty love will we summon to ensure the ending of this violence, this hate, this destruction of our Mother Earth, this grotesque inequality of wealth, this mad and ferocious drive to our end?

Here's what Donald Trump is not:

He is not us.

He is not all of us.

He is not the best of us.

He is not inevitable.

Let us take Trump at his word. Let him be our Unifier.

Keep Us Fed

Perhaps it is because, although it surprised her, it didn't really surprise her at all. She said, "Sexual, sexual molestation, couldn't be." First words, like someone punched her in the stomach. "I know he was violent toward you Eve, very violent, but he wouldn't do that." Then something rose up in me, a voice, a strength. I said, "Mother, if when I get finished, if when you hear what I have come to tell you, if then, you choose not to believe me, well that is your choice. I have no control over that. But that is not why I'm here. I am here because this happened to me, because it wrecked my life and I have been recovering from it for almost forty years. You need to know what happened. Because now there is a lie between us and that lie has prevented our love."

She got quiet. Her eyes were bulging. Her skin was beach-stained brown. Perhaps because she could not deny the signs that were there all through my childhood: the chronic kidney infections, the serious ongoing nightmares and night terrors from the time I was five, the hysterical fits, the alcoholism later, the anxiety attacks, the promiscuity, the dirty hair. I always had dirty, depressing hair. Perhaps it was the description of how he came in during the night, how I was the object that satisfied him, how I was afraid to speak, afraid to tell, because I loved him and knew he was bad, because it excited me to be so special, because I was sure my mother hated me because I had been forced to betray her and because I hated her because she never protected me and because he loved her and abandoned me. Perhaps it was because I could never get up in the morning, the terror, the disgust, the hatred of my body, my little genitals soiled beyond repair.

Perhaps it was because I had flown to Florida after not seeing her for years and there was a raging storm that had flooded the roads and we were sitting on her couch with the oriental pillows and the wild ocean getting closer and closer. "Did he penetrate . . . did he penetrate you?" Now, suddenly the most important question. Perhaps it was because she knew he could violently beat me, he could also invade me, that in the end it was about power and control. Perhaps it was because in spite of my best plans, I was weeping, tears bursting from my face like shrapnel. This story I was telling had completely corrupted and finished me. For thirty-nine years I'd been unraveling it and surviving it and finding me inside it and now I was telling it to her. Perhaps it was because I was always split between two worlds—the night child and the day child, the secret and the sun, the mother and the father. Perhaps it was because those worlds had just come together for the first time, in my mother's living room. Bone repair. Big human heal. Perhaps it was because as she sat weeping, believing me, I had a mother for the first time.

It took time for my mother's denial to melt away, but when it did, she broke down. She began to own things step by step. She admitted that she had never been my mother, that she had allowed the abuse, watched it, participated in it. She said she hadn't known about the incest, but she admitted that all the signs were there. She wept from guilt. She wept for my pain and she wept for her pain—all the years she had lived with a man who had terrorized her and controlled her and gotten her to allow the abuse of her children. She asked questions about the incest, specific questions. She asked what she could do to help me heal, to try and be my mother, to love me now, the way she didn't love me then.

That was the beginning. She started therapy. She came to visit. She asked me to tell her things, to talk about my rage toward her, to let her know. She read books about incest. She told her friends and her brother and my sister and brother what my father did to me. No one was surprised. She called with memories and validations. She confessed deeper and deeper guilt.

Two days ago, she called to tell me that she was trying to understand how she'd been able to allow my father to abuse me the way he did. She realized she was terrified of losing her economic comfort. She was a mother with three children and no real skills. She couldn't bear the idea of being poor again. Poor with three kids. So, she sacrificed me. That's what she said. You were my sacrifice.

In the center of a huge slab of concrete, surrounded by a pitch-black pool of water, there lies a naked girl-child, a little bloodied, a little bruised, almost lifeless. Keep us safe oh Lord. Keep us fed. Keep us comfortable. We offer her body to thee.

The Alchemy of Apology

2021
———

This was written as a sermon for the Middle Church in New York City at the invitation of the Reverend Dr. Jacqueline Lewis.

I come to you as many things. I come as a woman who has at times been lost and anxious and despaired, and I come to you as a woman who has known the deepest bliss, contentment, and love. I come as a woman who has opened myself to all genders, and a woman who has been terrified of intimacy. I come as an artist saved by the act of creation, and I come as an activist giving what I needed the most. I come as a friend and a mother and a sister and a daughter and a rebel. I come as a white person whose ancestral legacy is responsible for the murdering, stealing, pillaging, raping, and removing of the Indigenous who lived here, and four hundred years of slavery, lynchings, murder, rape of Black people. I come from Jewish ancestors erased in genocide. I come from the oppressed and the oppressor. The murderer and the murdered. These stories shame me and catalyze me every day. I come with mad hope and I come with outrage. I come with sorrow. I come with magic. I come with grief that feels so huge it could fill the oceans with my tears. I come knowing each one of us is divine and I come knowing we are wildly imperfect. I come as a seeking human being and I come as a know-it-all. I come as a white middle-class person who had all the economic and racial privileges and I come as a girl who was devastated by sexual violence beginning at five from that same father of privilege and then murderous violence that ravaged me until I left home at eighteen. I come to you with a heart breaking from the violence and hate of the world and I come to you as a woman who is forever moved by the generosity and kindness of the many. I come to you as a person who wonders deeply if we humans have a future here on earth and I come to as someone who will fight to the end to make sure we do. I come to you as a realist, and I come to you as a believer in miracles. I come to you as a woman who lives in the woods and worships trees and serves The Mother and I come to you as a city dweller searching for a way home. I come to talk about the alchemy of apology.

Some ground rules. This as an offering, not a prescription, not a must do, not the only way. It is an offering, period. Every survivor, every person has their own journey, their own process, their own timing, what works for one person may not work for another and what works at one moment of your life may not work at another. I am simply sharing my own experience, which is the only thing I truly trust. There may be things I write that are difficult and hard to hear.

As I said, my early years were brutal and full of terror and pain. My father sexually abused me from five to ten and after he stopped, he needed to erase what he had already destroyed so he physically and emotionally battered me, almost murdering me until I left home at eighteen.

This abuse altered the constitutional makeup of my entire being. It filled my cells and blood and body with terror, worry, guilt, and dread—that would in my teenage years and on until my sixties develop into all-encompassing self-hatred and anxiety. The abuse created infections in my body and seriously compromised my immune system. In my fifties I would get stage 3/4 uterine cancer. (I am miraculously totally well now for thirteen years.) The abuse froze me and made it almost impossible to concentrate or think. This had a terrible impact on my ability to study and learn. This reconfirmed my father's idea of me as a stupid person. The abuse made intimacy claustrophobic, made love foreign, made safety a pipe dream, and drew me constantly to dangerous situations and people in an attempt to master my past and my fear. The abuse led to addiction: alcohol, drugs, and sex.

I tell you all this not for your pity or sorrow. I tell you because when we talk about violence against women it is so abstract, so broad, we don't realize the specific detailed ways it impacts our lives and how many years, how much time it takes to rise from the ashes. I have been blessed that for my early years I was able to waitress and make enough money to survive. I was then doubly blessed that I made my way as a writer so I could afford to pay for the resources—like therapy—to help me lift the lid off that very dark period of my life. I know others are not so fortunate and I know if we lived in the world I dream of, we would take at least 70 percent of the money we spend on bombs and missiles and grenades and guns and war and killing and we would redirect it into a national trauma fund so that all those who are suffering from some kind of trauma, whether it be physical or sexual violence, ancestral violence, ableist, racial, or gender violence could have the means and resources and love and attention to recover. Can you imagine the outcome of a country that treated the trauma of its citizens rather than punishing them for being wounded or poor or mentally ill or unhoused or broke or deprived or angry or violent?

As I said, I have spent my life climbing out of the hole of this betrayal and terror, finding a way back into my body. My father died thirty-one years ago and for the years before he died and the years after I've been waiting for him to make a reckoning, to be accountable to make an apology.

So, I decided to write his apology in his voice with his words, to write a letter where he would say all the things I needed to hear.

The apology required time. It could not be rushed. My father, the one imagined, the one inside me had to spend days reliving his crime, mentally reenacting the details, feeling what it must have been like inside the daughter he abused. He had to strip away the hardness that prevented him from empathy—the indifference that rejected responsibility, rejected even the notion of the apology itself.

I asked him to remember my cries and pleading and to look back and see what my face looked like when he demeaned or insulted or grabbed or beat or raped me. I asked him to meditate and try to feel and experience what it was like inside my body as I experienced the terror, rage, claustrophobia, heartbreak, and betrayal. It had to be thorough. The liberation for both the perpetrator and the victim is in the details.

I have asked many women what justice would look like after they've been sexually abused or battered or incested or harassed. Some women demand punishment, prison time for their perpetrators, public exposure, loss of jobs, end of careers. Some women simply want their perpetrator to disappear forever. But many women I've spoken to say that in order to heal, in order to move on, what they want, and need is for their perpetrator to acknowledge the truth of what he has done. They want their perpetrator to recognize them as a full and real human being—to acknowledge the harm he has caused and to feel remorse and heartbreak. They need to see their perpetrator has taken responsibility for his actions and done extensive work to understand what made him commit this violence. They need to know the depth of his reckoning will prevent him from ever committing violence again.

What is an apology? It is a humbling. It is a loss of grandiosity and superiority. It is an admission of wrongdoings. It is a surrender. It is an equalizer. It's making true connection.

An apology is the antidote to convenient and infuriating forgetting that grips our families and country. Apologies rip open the lies, denial, myths, delusions that keep the violent story in place. An apology is a remembering, a public acknowledgment that what occurred actually did occur.

The powerful have been trained never to apologize. They make themselves the victims. That's what my father did. Even as he whipped me and threw me against walls, he was the victim, reminding me always how it hurt him more than it hurt me, how I was the reason he had to behave like this. I made him do it. He had no choice.

Some accused men have lost jobs and careers and reputations. Some have gone to prison. But even when they come forward to describe what they have learned since being accused, they don't say the words, acknowledge the specificity of their crimes. They don't trace the history of their own stories or development of distortions in their own psyches that would at least attempt to make sense of their brutality. They don't investigate the system of patriarchy and privilege that allowed, encouraged, and gave them cover for this violence. They don't wrestle down their demons and expose vulnerability. Instead, when called out, they speak of their own pain and loss and misfortune steeped in self-pity.

I have read no words of any man accused of sexual abuse who has taken the painstaking steps to self-revelation, who has done the treacherous work of owning his actions, searching his history to trace the seeds and reasons for his crime, in facing his violence, in speaking the words. In making the apology. And I do not know if it is simply ignorance or inability or shame or male entitlement or refusal or arrogance or that men are simply unable to face so much pain or they have been so trained to hold on to their pride and power to the final hour. My father says in the book that for a man to apologize is to be a traitor to men. Once one man admits he was wrong, the whole story begins to collapse.

So many of us have been waiting. I think of brave Anita Hill and Christine Blasey Ford. I think of the comfort women in Korea who were kidnapped and raped by Japanese soldiers during World War II, standing every Wednesday at vigils for thirty years, waiting, waiting for the apology to come. Most of them have died now, the rest are old and failing. They have never heard the words and they will never rest.

We have devoted our lives waiting for this truth to be uncovered because it lives in the center of everything we are and are not. It's the stoplight in our nervous systems. Without this accounting we cannot go on. For a lingering lie is an undeniable stain that controls and defines. That lie is like a cancer cell that first invades and then spreads through the whole system.

And even when we appear to go on, even when we move our bodies forward and go to our jobs and feed our children, we can never be whole. Because without justice there is no freedom, there is no integrity; there is no full life.

It's the system that has to change, the fundamental beliefs, the values, the central idea. The question is how do we address patriarchy, the paradigm that underlies all of this violence? We have to get under the story in order to uproot it rather than continuing to ram up against it. We have to offer a doorway rather than a locked cell. We have to move from humiliation to revelation, from curtailing behavior to changing it, from containing perpetrators to calling them to reckoning.

And the truth is, the system of patriarchy is as poisonous to the winners as it is to the losers. As devastating to the men who are severed from their hearts and tenderness as it is to the women who suffer terrible violence as a result of that separation. Women spend their time recovering from sexual violence and men spend their lives covering for it and both these things empty and take our years. The truest healing heals the victim and perpetrator at once because both are forever caught inside the same story. Punishment in itself cannot offer this healing.

Many men are afraid and confused now. They don't know how to act. And of course, having this new awareness is a good thing. But being on guard does not necessarily mean being aware of the issues, does not ensure being educated or taking responsibility or exploring your inner depths to see where you are sexist or culpable or how your past actions have hurt someone and where you need to make repairs. Being on guard means being sure you don't screw up, make a mistake, or get caught. It's a punishment response. You're in fear, on hold, suspended. It is not a state of mind in which you are open or vulnerable or where you can learn or change.

I believe this deeper process can be rooted in apology. For an apology is an excavation, insisting that the perpetrator go beneath the surface, be willing to mine the layers of truth and guilt hidden beneath each new revelation. An apology is both a method and a practice. The act itself holds the possibility of transformation, of liberation. When it is offered, as it's received the authentic apology creates an alchemical reaction, a physical, spiritual, psychological dissolving of the offense and rancor, bitterness, revenge, or hate. This is actually what forgiveness feels like. As Emma Goldman once said, "Before we can forgive one another, we have to understand one another."

We need to teach apology the way we teach prayer for it is in fact a practice, and it requires practice to get it right. It demands the devotion and concentration of prayer. It demands the vulnerability of that petition and the humility. Each one of us humans is flawed, and imperfect, engaged hopefully in uplifting our souls and evolving our humanity. I believe apology is the medicine, the salve that cleanses and fortifies and allows us to continue on. But it must be taught. It must be practiced.

There are four essential steps to an apology.

One: Investigate your own history and look at what led you to act the way you acted. What went into making you the kind of person, a man, a white person, able-bodied, a settler, who was capable of such harm. Discovering the origin, the history of our action is key to making sure it doesn't happen again.

Two: Admit in detail what you have done. Broad strokes will not be effective, that is, I am sorry if I hurt you. I'm sorry if I made you feel bad. Freedom is in the details for both the person making and receiving the apology. I am sorry I threw you down the stairs. Sorry I tore you clothes off and didn't listen to your voice screaming for me to stop. The more detailed the apology the more freedom will ensue.

Three: Feel and understand the impact of your harm on your victim. This requires empathy, climbing inside the feelings and being of the person you have been mean or cruel to.

Four: Taking fully responsibility for what you have done, making the apology. All of these steps indicating that it would be impossible for you to do anything like this again.

I hear survivors often being told they "need to forgive their perpetrators and move on." I worry how we use forgiveness, how somehow, we skip the vital piece of reckoning and accounting before any form of true forgiveness can occur. In many religions there is confession, there is an admitting of wrongs that generates forgiveness. The onus is not on the victim to forgive. This feels like a forced mandate, and without the discourse and action of the apology it can be a hollow and inorganic act not truly releasing the victim or the perpetrator from guilt and rage.

Writing *The Apology* was one of the most painful, difficult, and liberatory things I have ever done. I had to enter the wound. I had to, as Dr. Cornel West brilliantly describes, "make a courageous, creative, unflinching look at catastrophe." I had to remake myself and my idea of myself and break the vice of my lifelong identity being victim to my father's perpetrator. I had to paint my father in more diverse and intricate colors. I had to enter his pain, his history, and I had to grieve for him. I discovered that my father, my perpetrator, was part of me, that I know him in some ways better than I know myself and that I have been in conscious or unconscious dialogue with him inside me my whole life. And I came to the startling realization that I could change who he was inside me, how he behaved. He owned his terrible deeds, he felt my pain, he evidenced awareness and remorse. He took responsibility and he apologized. He went from abuser and monster to vulnerable and hurting human being. And, for the first time, I feel genuinely free.

I realize even the desire for the apology is a tall order. It would mean at the very least a remaking of human consciousness. It would mean becoming vulnerable and lost, and could potentially mean a radical change of identity and position. But what it could also mean is being involved in a process that has the possibility of bringing us into a time, where the tyranny of misogyny, which has robbed men of their hearts and tenderness and humanity, is transformed into a time of equality, peace, and loving connection between all people.

Our imagination is our most powerful weapon. We can conjure the dead. We can rewrite their stories. We can make them see us as they have never seen us. We can get them to reveal themselves and see themselves and we can transform the underlying narrative that has us caught in a cycle of violence, punishment, more violence.

I often ask myself what I am doing here on this earth. My answer is simple. I am here to get free. Free of my rancor, free of my pain, free of racism, free of ableism, transphobia, homophobia, and reversing the legacy I carry as a white person, free of prejudice and unkindness, free of self-loathing, free of my desire to hurt, free to live in my body, free of jealousy, ego, free of not feeling like enough, free of not feeling that I have enough, free of comparison, free to be my authentic self. Free to serve that which is divine. Only then can I manifest my real purpose, our real purpose which is to love. And I don't mean a sentimental touchy-feely kind of love. I mean a fierce love, a love born in the alchemy of the wound, of the shadow, of the shamanic fire of the true and radiant apology.

Finding Your Place

2016
———

The first time I awakened to the depth of my own disassociation
from place was in Rawalpindi, Pakistan, during the years of the
Bosnian War. I had gone to a refugee camp there to meet and
interview a group of Bosnian refugees who had been taken in
by the Pakistani government, generously offering sanctuary to
fellow Muslims. The people were from small villages in Bosnia
that had been under siege by Serbian forces. Some had lost
family members, some had been raped. Some were recovering
from violent injuries. Everyone was traumatized, uprooted, and
dislocated. The conditions of the camp were very basic and difficult: no clean water, overwhelming heat, lots of illness. Hardly
anyone spoke English. The customs and even the practice of
religion in Pakistan were foreign to Muslims from Europe who
up until the war had never been deeply religious or aware of
themselves as Muslim.

The Bosnians were sick, lonely, depressed, but what possessed them all was almost a viral homesickness.

There were about five hundred people there and many were from a town called Donji Vakuf in central Bosnia. An older man from the town had decided to do something to relieve his community of their desperate longing for home. He built a model of Donji Vakuf with streets and mosque and churches, cafés and town halls and a tower that stood in the center with clocks on all four sides so the people coming from every direction would know what time it was. It was a stunning replica, laid out on the stone floor. The group would make a strong pot of Bosnian coffee, grab their cigarettes, and sit around the model talking, complaining, and gossiping as if they were returned to their precious town. It seemed to bring them back to life. They would point to various spots on the model, and this would instigate reminiscences and stories that would fill the morning and the afternoon.

I was astonished to see the depth of their attachment to a place and how even being near a facsimile of it restored their good natures and happiness.

One day the community discovered the tower of the replica was missing. There was a young woman in the camp who had a serious case of epilepsy. It was very hot in Pakistan and each time she went into the sun she had gone into multiple seizures, so she had been relegated to her bed with the shades pulled and had become seriously depressed. It was eventually discovered that she had taken the tower into her bed and had been sleeping with it, clutched to her chest like a puppy. It was bringing her deep comfort and had lifted her spirits immensely. The community decided she needed the tower more than they did.

I was in awe, and to be honest, perplexed. I had never known anything resembling such a love and attachment to a place. I had never missed a place.

Up until this point in my life, place was something I fled and was fleeing. Place was where bad things happened. Place was the castle of a madman where you were caught for eternity, at his whim, delivered daily into his cruelty with no reprieve. Place was anxiety and terror. It held the nightmares and the smells of abuse. Staying still in one place would allow him to find you. I did not want to be found.

I wanted to move and not stop moving. I wanted to be as far from the murderous suburbs as possible. I wanted a permanent exit from normal and family and home. I was a psychological nomad, never landing physically or emotionally, never staying, never truly available, frustrating lovers and partners who sensed they could never have me even when I was there, and the truth is, they couldn't. I romanticized my exile, made myself believe I was the one who had determined it, called it independence, freedom. To some degree that was true, but ultimately underlying it all was fear of place, terror of settling, of being had. On the deepest level it wasn't a real choice. Fight or flight. I was in a life of flight.

The first real apartment I lived in in New York City, I moved the bed into the living room, as I hated bedrooms. I hated that room tucked away in the dark where most of the violations of my childhood had occurred. I hated dining rooms where most of the beatings and assaults had begun. I never saw where I lived as the place I stayed. I saw it like a train station, something I was passing through, a place that kept my things when I returned from escaping. It is why the city was so appealing. Although it is a location, it was a transient one for me.

What determines place? Community perhaps, nature, a sense of belonging, commitment to the people who live with you and by you, commitment to be a good steward to the earth that supports you. I think of the astonishing poem by David Whyte. I have this particular verse painted on my kitchen wall.

This is the bright home,
in which I live,
this is where
I ask
my friends
to come,
this is where I want
to love all the things
it has taken me so long
to learn to love.

This is the temple
of my adult aloneness
and I belong
to that aloneness
as I belong to my life.

People mistake nationalism for love of place. Nationalism is dedication to an ideology, a righteousness, a patriotism that declares one nation better than others. Loving a place has nothing to do with hierarchy or competition. The depth of love for your place organically connects you to all places. Your place in your streets, on your block, in the forest, in the web of life, which is part of the whole organism of life. This organism is without boundaries or borders. The deeper you ground in one place, the more connected you are to all places. The deeper you fall in love with trees around you, the deeper your love for all trees.

John Berger wrote:

> This century, for all its wealth and with all its communication systems, is the century of banishment. Eventually perhaps the promise of which Marx was the great prophet, will be fulfilled, and then the substitute for the shelter of a home will not just be your personal names, but our collective conscious presence in history, and we will live again at the heart of the real. Despite everything I can imagine it.

Our cities are flooded with the banished. Those regarded as problems or black sheep in their families, ostracized and fleeing hate and punishment, fleeing persecution, war, poverty, hatred, landlessness, searching for jobs and safety.

In a global capitalist system, every place is for ransacking and conquest, every place for potential expansion and exploitation. Place becomes commodified, a thing to be acquired, serving the interests of the corporations and the very rich. And as lands get destroyed by imperialistic wars, climate crisis brought about by plundering through extraction and devastating pollution of waters, earth and air, and massive unemployment brought about globalization, more people are forced to flee in search of safe ground and jobs.

Global capitalism not only escalates a mass exodus from place, it relies on it. When people are separated from their homes, from their bases, families, from their grounding in culture, farms, their rivers, their tradition, community, and continuity, they are destabilized, vulnerable to exploitation, oppression, death, and tyranny. The earth is where we draw our strength. The community is where we are shaped and held, validated, known and protected.

Today, as I write, the Trump administration has issued a ban on Muslims coming into the United States from seven Muslim countries, Iraq, Syria, Iran, Libya, Somalia, Sudan, and Yemen. One of the underpinnings of America, a country made of immigrants, has been our willingness to offer people throughout the world safety and harbor, a place to land and rebuild. Now the corporates, the racists, and the rich who rule America are devastating this as well. And to heap insult upon injury, most of the countries we are banning are countries we have been part of destroying through imperialist interventions. We are banishing those we are responsible for bombing. Double banishment, dystopian banishment. Banishments inside of banishment.

I left the city and moved to the woods. I do not take this blessing lightly.

I walked outside this morning and the pond mist was melting and the moon was high, and the sun was finding its way through. Maybe it was the rain all yesterday. Maybe it was the sudden warmth in January. Maybe it was the luminous copper of the slumbering wheat fields, or the snow that had melted and the suddenly unburdened grass, green and waiting, or maybe it was the clear stone path, dark with wet. Whatever it was, it was as if earth tore off the winter veil for a brief moment and revealed a world beneath. There was a clarity to everything, an exactness, an order. As I walked, a word began to echo through my mind, "place place, you have arrived at a place. You have found your place. This is your place." I wanted to be loyal to this place. And make altars to this place. I wanted to marry this place (and

I have never been a fan of marriage). I wanted to tattoo it on my arm and give myself fully to it and never travel or leave this place again. I didn't want to miss a thing. Not a morning of mist or sullen skies that go on until four and then drop over a cliff of darkness. This place I now have to get back to, that I am beginning to learn as deeply as I know my own hands.

To agree to marry a place means not living in the ever possible, the ever searching. It means settling as in settling down. It means accepting limitations, being humbled. It means landing.

Global capitalism has turned land into real estate. Its rapacious hunger has forced the Indigenous off their sovereign lands and is destroying their water and air. It has forced migrants to leave their families to cross borders to work for slave wages. It has been responsible for bombing millions who now drift in armies of the lost, the broken and bewildered. It has birthed a wealthy jet-setting class who see land not as place but as proof of their wealth and status.

Place is real. Having one means not grabbing more than your share. It means the satisfaction of enough. It means meeting yourself and wrestling down the demons kept at bay by your wandering. It means being a steward to where you stand.

As a wave of authoritarianism and hate sweeps across the country and much of the world, as an openly predatory mindset is aggressively asserted in every aspect of our lives, our greatest defense will be our singular commitment to guarding and protecting all that is sacred: our earth, refugees and immigrants, marginalized communities, our principles, our values, our friendships, our human bond. This can only happen if we are willing to release the tentacles of our endless longing and grasping. Our disposability is only made impossible if we are able to root ourselves in the real, in the humble, in a covenant with place and a commitment to struggling so that no person is ever forced out of their sacred place by war, greed, or climate disaster.

This house, this land is bigger than my own worry or concerns. I am small in it, right sized. I belong to the massive guardian locust trees who shield me as I rest. I belong to the worn rocks where the water flows heavy after rain. I belong to the shocking red cardinal at my feeder in the snow and the black snake that visits in the late afternoon and spreads out lazily on the stone wall.

I belong to the pieces of crystal ice falling and making diamond magic on the limestone path. I belong to the pines and oaks and willows. I belong to the nakedness of winter. I belong to the stars and skeletal branches draped in raspberry haze tainted by a blood moon. I belong to the great-tailed grackles that arrive in hundreds with their high-pierced whistles and fill the limbs of the mulberry tree with witchy wonder. I belong to the invisible mice chewing at my candles and racing in the eaves late into the night. I belong to the ancient snapping turtle who arduously climbs the hill that particular day in May and then effortlessly slips her weathered body into the pond. I belong to all this and this belonging is the balm.

Roses the Size of Teacup Saucers

CITY OF JOY, BUKAVU, DEMOCRATIC REPUBLIC OF THE CONGO,
SEPTEMBER 2018

For Mama C

It's been over two years since I've been able to visit City of Joy. No luck with visas combined with high insecurity. The war quietly and invisibly rages on, but City of Joy, like so much else in the Congo, cannot be deterred. It is fertile, alive, intense, insistent, and thriving in spite of everything the world has to throw at it. Now I'm finally back. Here's what's changed:

Saplings have become tall trees.

A tiny orange bush is now heavy with oranges.

A garden has become a small forest.

Roses are now the size of teacup saucers.

Untested staff have risen to the occasion and are highly trained and totally effective professionals.

Women, once skinny, starving, and traumatized, are full bodied and strong.

Women who passed through the first class, once defenseless and brutalized, are trained guards defending other women.

Girls have turned the stones in their hearts and pasts to flowers.

Once boring wooden office desks are chicly covered in swirling madly colored pagnes.

A meditation hut has been erected where the perfect breeze wafts through layers of stunning tapestry.

There are silent zones to pause and reflect and feel peace.

Victims have become survivors who have become leaders.

Military wives, abandoned by the government, who live in the surrounding dilapidated camp have become active members of the City of Joy community. Two have been hired as staff.

1,117 women have graduated.

They have gone on to:

lead in their communities

run farm collectives

go to school
recruit other women for City of Joy
live at V-World Farm now and work as farmers
demand their rights
become nurses, teachers, herbalists, social workers,
healers, organizers
refuse men who are not their equals.
At V-World Farm:

There are two hundred farmers and workers employed. Three hundred families are living off a gifted piece of land. The surrounding community is part of the project.

The houses for ninety women are built and stunning.

There is a state-of-the-art theater.

The pigs and lambs and goats and bunnies have multiplied.

Tilapia are harvested by the tons. Food from V-World Farm feeds the women at City of Joy.

Moringa grows and avocados and pineapple and papaya.

And sweet potatoes and tons of rice and fennel.

And a wild accidental red flower.

This is the new paradigm manifested on earth. A world where staff are filled with so much joy, they literally stop their morning, take off their shoes to dance. Where crying is invited, where ideas are expansive, where love is the central verb. City of Joy is the diamond in the rough. The rising citadel in the center of war and brokenness. Where the radiance of those who have turned their suffering into power spreads in all directions. Where miracles are catalyzed by the transfiguration of pain into joy. Here's an example.

There were a pair of twins, Cikuru (first born) and Cito (second born). When they were three years old, the militias entered their village, and they were forced to run. Their father was murdered, and they became separated from their mother. Then they were taken away from each other. They were each taken in by separate families who treated them like servants. They were each raped several times. They were each abandoned and re-abandoned. They had not seen each other for fifteen years. One did not remember she had a sister. One had a vague memory. They were each referred to City of Joy. On the boat to travel there, other girls on the boat noticed that there were two girls on the boat who looked shockingly alike. They found each other and discovered they were twin sisters. They found the part that was missing. They found their family. They both went through six months at City of Joy together. They both purged their pain and released their stones. They moved to V-World Farm. They work there now and go to school. They cry when they speak of their mother. They have pledged never to leave each other again in this life. They are saving their money to buy land and a house. They are sisters. Rising.

To All Those Who Dare Rob Us of Our Bodily Choice

MAY 6, 2022

I ask you:

What is it about our bodies that make you so afraid,
    so insecure, so cruel and punishing?
    Is it their singular autonomy or mere existence?
    Is it their capacity for immense and unending pleasure — orgasms that can multiply orgasms inside orgasms. Is it our skin?
Is it our desire?
    Is it our openness that rattles you and reminds you of where
you are closed?
    Is it the pure strength of our bodies that allows us to bleed and
birth and bend and carry and continue
    on in spite of all the ways you have reduced us and
    objectified us, humiliated us and disrespected us and tried to
shape us into baby-making machines?

Our strength that is inherent and doesn't need to prove itself or show off or rely on weapons or violence to control and terrorize? Doesn't need to abolish laws, or lie to become Supreme Court judges or president or rig the decks when they get there.

Do you know this power? Can you imagine it? A power that comes from respecting life, caring for others before oneself, holding communities together?

Do you think we are naive enough to believe that you are motivated by your care for life when you have shown so little respect for it and us? Instead you spend your days unraveling and resisting all that makes life possible for those mothers and people with babies you claim to protect—fighting against free universal health care, parental paid leave, and child allowance. Where's your outrage that this country has the highest maternal mortality rates in the developed world?

Do you think we have forgotten that some of those who are making the most crucial decisions about millions of our bodies (Kavanaugh and Thomas) and the one (Trump) who chose three of the people on the court currently making these decisions, are men who have been accused of raping other women's bodies, harassing women's bodies, humiliating and proudly bragging about grabbing the genitals of women's bodies? Why would we ever trust them to come near our bodies, let alone determine the future of them?

What is it about our bodies that makes you think you have the right to invade them, determine them, control and legislate them, violate and force them to do anything against their will?

Perhaps you mistake our generosity for weakness, our patience for passivity, our vulnerability for fragility.

This might be why you are unable to see that there is no

chance in hell that we are ever going back. This is not a law yet and we will never accept this ruling.

Perhaps because you have never known what it is like to have your body controlled by the vindictive anonymous state, to be raped and forced to keep your baby at twelve years old, to be so desperate that you destroy your uterus with a hanger or bleed to death in a back alley, you do not understand that once you have tasted the sweetness of freedom, of choice, once you have come to know your body as your own, once you have freed yourself and felt the expanse of your body, the aliveness in every pore that rises from autonomy, there is no way you will ever give that up. Ever.

And because you do not know this, you do not know how dangerous we are, how organized we are, how willing we are to go to any lengths to preserve our freedom.

It's been fifty years. We have summoned our due. We actually have bank accounts now. We have credit cards and we can buy a house. We can serve on juries. We hold offices and are lawyers. We write for newspapers and we run them. We host TV shows and direct movies. We run hospitals and universities and non-profits and write plays about vaginas and books about fascists and fascism. We can't be tossed aside.

This is our world now. And these are our bodies.

We know what you are up to—this is just the beginning of your diabolical plan to rob us of contraception and marriage equality and civil rights and voting rights and on and on. This is all part of your desperation to prevent the future that is on the verge of being born—a future where we know our past and begin to reckon with it, a future where we teach critical race theory and the truth about white supremacy and sexism and transphobia. A future where we care for our earth and devote our lives to protecting air and water and forests and animals and all living things, a future where people have autonomy over their bodies and wombs and gender and marry who they want to and don't marry if they don't want to and have babies if they want to and don't have babies if they don't want to and despite all your lies, strategies, and devious ways you are simply never going to stop us.

You have unleashed our fury, our solidarity, our unity.

We know that our future and everything we have fought for is at stake. I am willing to lay my body down for this freedom, for every freedom and I know there are multitudes who will do the same.

Eve's Revolution

2018

_____

For Monique

This is a speech I delivered for the Bioneers Summit Conference in 2014. The theme was "Growing the Movement."

Let me go back to Eve, first woman, Adam, serpent, apple, garden, God. I take you back there because that's where this story begins.

I have been obsessed with Eve my whole life. First of course, it was once my name. And for a six-year-old it seemed ridiculously impossible to be named Eve. She was responsible for not only the downfall of paradise, expulsion, sin, shame but death itself. Names like myths determine a lot.

In a deep sense I belonged to that story of Adam and Eve. It was like a tectonic plate at the bedrock of my consciousness, engendering how I saw myself and how I behaved in the world. And I believe that story consciously or unconsciously has shaped a great deal of humanity.

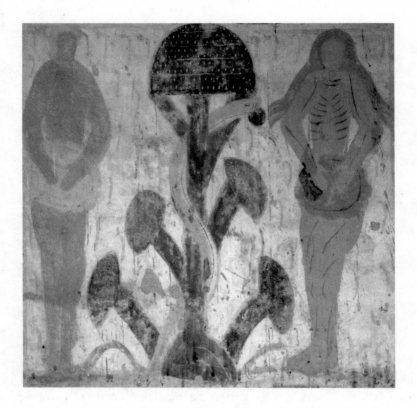

How many of us feel as if we are fallen women/people out of the gate—our inherent credibility or value erased upon birth. How many of us are controlled by the debilitating terror that any form of disobedience or independence will lead to social exclusion and damnation? How many of us feel cursed for our curiosity, forbidden to know what we know, living amid a culture constantly manifesting a pathological and patronizing disdain for our instincts, delegitimizing our intuition or belittling anything that might lead to a deeper, more embodied intelligence. The myth of Eve has served as eternal warning, an electric fence around our psyches zapping our impulses to revolt or question. I don't know about you, but the serpent has figured highly in my life, in the form of lovers, sex, drugs, rock and roll. I think many of us have been constantly ingesting things that are stand-ins for apples but always with a sense of being wrong. Our life force or hunger to be, our erotic impulses, have been distorted through this cellular shame and distrust.

Although this dominant story seems to rule our conscious life, if we stop and listen, we know there has been another story gnawing at our collective subconscious, another idea of the archetypal, mythic Eve.

I have read biographies of Eve and many of the feminist reinterpretations. My thought and vision of course rests inside and draws strength and particulars from them. Some have seen Eve as setting off to make the world according to her own experience, some see Eve as deeply identified with her sexuality, others see her as more intelligent, more compelling and confident, coveting wisdom.

I think it is crucial how we see Eve. She was in theory the first woman, the mother of life. And although she is a character in a parable, we know myths rule our existence, determine the walls of the stories we live in and the barriers of the ones we would like to construct. They become the architecture of our actions and lives. So, I am here today to present you with another story about Eve. I speak of her as archetype more than religious figure. I speak of her as one of many feminine archetypes who have had deep influence over our lives.

Eve ate the apple because, like many of us, she was trying to remember the other story, the story before the trauma of brainwashing and massacres. The story before they shoved things into our sacred holes and cut the tips of our clitorises where divinity lives. Before they shaved our furry nests and choked the throat of our songs. Before they called us hysterical and intense and emotional, before they beat boys for crying and wanting to wear dresses. Before they stoned us for uttering the words of our mothers and drilled down into us to rob us of our moist and fertile secrets. Before Eve was made to believe she was taken from a rib, before she was forced to be obedient. Before she stopped dancing as and in the undulations of stars and moon, before she stopped dancing, before she buried her powers to heal with touch and see the future and become one with earth. Before she knew how to pleasure herself over and over and over forever and men knew they were there to serve that pleasure because as she was pleasured they and the world were pleasured over and over forever. Before she was embarrassed by joy. Before she apologized for her heart and stopped respecting the size of its brain, before she disqualified her opinions and apologized for her insatiable curiosity. Before childbirth became punishment and love and service to a man became mandatory. Before she swallowed her rage and choked her voice. Before men established god the father at the top. Before there was a top. Before the earth was treated as the wretched wild. Before when it was life generating life in all directions. Eve ate the apple because the trajectory of her hunger was our way back and the apple was the fruit of memory, the medicine of recall, the aphrodisiac of original connection. Eve ate the apple to regain her powers, to know what she knew before she was held hostage in the wrong garden.

The Bible tells us that God said to Adam and Eve: "You may surely eat of every tree of the garden, but the tree of the knowledge of good and evil you shall not eat, for in the day that you eat of it you shall surely die."

Certain scholars such as Gordon Wasson, Carl Ruck, and Clark Heinrich have written that the mythological apple is a symbolic substitution for entheogenic *Amanita muscaria* mushrooms. You know, the red ones with the white polka dots? When we look at an illustration of Adam and Eve from the thirteenth century, we see a surprising image. Undeniably, the tree of knowledge is pictured as a mushroom here and the serpent is wrapped around it. The serpent, who was Eve's inner deeper knowing, said eat the red fruit and you will not die and by the way, God lied, they didn't die. The serpent said your eyes will be open, and I believe their eyes were opened and the apple or the mushroom connected them directly to divinity without the intermediary of God, the father.

So, Eve ate the apple and came into her full independent erotic self and heart—then generously offered this transformation to Adam and immediately punishment, shame, guilt, and oppression descended upon them. They were expelled and have been wandering inside us and outside us trying to remember ever since. Eve was cast out as she opened the door to the deeper knowing, and we must all be okay outside our father's garden, outside his house, outside the world of disembodied intelligence, we must all be visionary nomads, exiled from the hierarchy and ready to find one another and create the new world, which is really just remembering the world from which we came.

Eve ate the apple to remember the time before our souls were militarized and straightjacketed by religions that rendered us defeated, guilty, sinful, waiting for someone or something usually a father god or consumer god coming to rescue us or redeem us or protect us when in fact there was never anything to be rescued from except those who in our name were committing wars and violence protecting us. Eve who knew we didn't need a soldier of paradise or mythic corporate daddy who has occupied our imagination and our days into passive projects of waiting waiting waiting while those who use his name pillage and hoard the goods. Eve who knew paradise didn't need to be carried in on a white horse or descend in an illumined cloud because in fact paradise was already here and our project rather than waiting for paradise to be delivered was instead to develop the capacity, desire, and vision to recognize and appreciate the paradise already here. The paradise not constructed on hierarchy and competition and domination and greed but on connection and mutual cooperation. The paradise that grew from the earth herself delivering everything humans needed and beyond anything they could have dreamed.

And God said Adam and Eve will have dominion over the earth. Subdue her and multiply. Eve knew in her body memory that this was the greatest misconception and violation and would send the story of the world exactly where it has gone to dominate and occupy and subdue our mother our earth who was not only feeding us but who was in fact US. That this separation from her lacerated by the brutal power-hungry conceptual machete of those who turned the snake into the devil, Eve into the initiator of original sin, and the earth herself into a mad devouring and terrifying demon who had to be tamed and controlled. This separation that exiled us from the inherent life-sustaining umbilicus of our green mother left us hungry and searching to return to her body, our bodies. That hunger which has made us vulnerable to tyranny, more concerned with acceptance and approval than resisting the ongoing violations and atrocities committed on humanity and the earth. That hunger which has led to dramatic and contemporary addictions, drugs, food, shopping, sex, all overcompensating for the desperation to be one with nature and, in turn, ourselves.

This separation was enacted and enforced by violence on our bodies because as Eve knew, it is in our bodies where the memory lives. The only way to forget was to force us out of our bodies. To rape them, beat them, torture, bully them, threaten them, and to commit the same heinous acts on our Mother Earth while forcing us to be what felt like helpless spectators of this holy destruction, and after in our horror we not only fled our own bodies but the violated and stigmatized body of the mother and in her place turned in our desperation and terror for protection and sustenance to the perpetrators themselves.

Eve asked neither Adam nor God for permission. She knew what she had to do, and I believe she must have known at least instinctively what could follow. She knew she risked their disapproval and somewhere in her she must have known her legacy, legitimacy, and name could be ruined, and she could be expelled from the comforting mirage and garden of patriarchy, but may I remind us this didn't stop her. She was our whistleblower, knowing she was in the wrong garden. She ate the apple, chewed and swallowed into her body, absorbed it into her bloodstream like a kind of medicine like a kind of potion, a sweet red flesh ball of remembering. She ate the apple because her hunger for justice, ecstasy, connection, pleasure, equality, and love was massively alive in her. Her hunger for connection to the erotic and as Audre Lorde writes in her visionary piece *The Uses of the Erotic*:

> As women, we have come to distrust that power which
> rises from our deepest and non-rational knowledge. We
> have been warned against it all our lives by the male

world, which values this depth of feeling enough to
keep women around in order to exercise it in the service of men, but which fears this same depth too much
to examine the possibilities of it within themselves. Of
course, women so empowered are dangerous.

Eve is alive in us, her hunger for the memories, she is in our
mother's body and we are on the brink of THE remembering.

How do we remember? What will jigger the flashbacks, images, and sensations?

First, we must openly unashamedly eat the apple. This
involves ingesting all that catalyzes and provokes vision and
imagination. It means educating ourselves and looking deeper
into the stories and myths designed and sustained by the powers
that be. Reintroducing ritual, poetry, time, human connection,
plant medicines, opening the box, learning the data, touching
the mystical, coming out of denial, coming into our bodies,
touch, dance, sex, trusting what we know, not asking permission,
defying authority. It means trusting our methods of remembering. Let me take a minute to talk about dance and One Billion
Rising. As many of you know, one of out of three women on the
planet will be raped or beaten in her lifetime. That's a billion
women. Almost ten years ago we invited the women of the
world and all the men who loved them to rise and dance to end
violence against women. It was extraordinary what happened.
Survivors and activists immediately responded and almost two
hundred countries and millions of people rose and danced.
But there were the skeptics, particularly in the media and cor-
poratized institutions who kept asking in patronizing sarcastic
ways why dance, what does dancing do, as if the ramblings
and operations of their so-called empirically based empire had

delivered us another world other than this one on the brink of human extinction.

I want to talk about the power of dancing, the power of state and domestic traumatized bodies collectively releasing and expanding and joining and resisting. Dancing invited people of all genders to reclaim and reenergize public space, spun and splashed creative and compassionate and determined energy in every direction. It made violence against women a front-page issue, allowed for autonomy and local organizing and global solidarity. It evoked demands for justice across a swath of intersectional issues, understanding that violence toward women cannot be separated from all the other violence whether it be economic, environmental, racial, gender. It added joy to the ingredients of our resistance and by doing so added sexuality and evoked the mystical and intangible, producing what seemed like miracles: construction workers in Peru who made sexual harassment–free construction sites. It educated one hundred thousand rickshaw drivers in India on gender violence and they now have signs on their rickshaws that read: My religion is respecting women.

It forced the government of the Philippines to protect the girls in the Payatas, the dumpsites where they were being forced to sell their bodies in order to scavenge. It freed hundreds of women from prison in Zimbabwe who were being held for passion crimes, it inspired men throughout the Congo to write a declaration of solidarity to end violence against women and girls and then follow it up with a national gathering of men. It joined with restaurant workers fighting to end substandard pay, which directly licensed the highest level of sexual harassment in any industry. It brought in women and men in prison who wrote songs about ending rape and honoring women. It led Haitian actors to perform *The Vagina Monologues* in Kreyòl in the Haitian parliament. It bodily and boldly insisted on the implementation of laws to prevent sexual violence, broke taboos, and compelled women to strip naked in Byron Bay, Australia, and dance themselves collectively into the sea. It compelled workers to dance at factories in front of corporations. Women rose in churches, at the International Criminal Court. It changed laws and forced the implementation of others, but mainly it allowed cisgender, transgender, nonbinary people, and men to come back into their bodies, to reclaim public space so they, like Eve, would begin to remember the world we know inside us that we must manifest outside us.

It escalated ecstatic revolt.

For years a certain scene at the end of Milton's *Paradise Lost* has haunted me. The archangel Michael is standing with Adam and Eve at the edge of the garden of Eden moments before their expulsion. He says to them, "Good out of evil will be a higher good then ere before." For years I took this to mean that we needed Eve to commit the sin of curiosity and disobedience. We needed Eve to bring an end to paradise because good without a knowledge of evil is a lesser good than good that overcomes evil. But I think Milton got it wrong. I think Eve already knew the higher good. I think she had the knowledge, like us in her body. She just needed to get out of that system, stop tiptoeing around that punishing and oppressive garden in order to get enough distance from the terror and trauma and terrorizing Father, state, corporate machine, get around like-minded people, get enough confidence and support to remember the first story. By the way, this was one of the central and most brilliant functions of Occupy Wall Street—to have a public subversive place for group remembering and redesigning. We need many more of them. We need them everywhere. Gardens of reimagination.

We are stuck in the patriarchal contaminated capitalist devastated garden, obeying the corporate daddy god still living as if he had our interest at heart, as if this so- called paradise without reflection or awareness in a somnolent state, seductive consumerism, near totalitarian surveillance, a corporately owned media, celebrity void culture, internet voyeurism and bullying were real or keeping us safe. Eve knew it was a mirage. She craved the real garden, the original garden before the father god implanted his hierarchy and the violence and the threat of punishment needed to sustain it.

I have just finished a wonderful new biography of Emma Goldman by Vivian Gornick. At one time Goldman was known as the most dangerous woman in America. A title we should all aspire to. An anarchist, a revolutionary. She is most famous for her quote "If I can't dance, I am not coming to your revolution." In the biography Gornick writes:

> Felt is the operative word. Emma always claimed that the ideas of anarchism were of secondary use if grasped only with reasoning intelligence. It was necessary to feel them in every fiber like a flame, a consuming fever, an elemental passion. Goldman's radicalism: an impassioned faith lived in the nervous system, that feelings were everything. If revolutionaries gave up sex and art while they were making the revolution she said they would be devoid of joy. Without joy human beings cease being human.

How do we build movements that are grown from loving life, fighting for life, love, pleasure, and joy?

How do we make radical outrageous pushing-the-edge art and music that mainlines our thinking and passions into the masses? How do we keep evolving and surprising and deepening—getting closer and closer to the root? How do we shut up and serve? Be more concerned with expanding than branding. Find resources for those without access to resources without controlling how they use them. Stop using money as a weapon but realize if you have some money to give away you are lucky, not special, and no one needs to jump through hoops for it because you don't have a hoop, you have money.

Eve was a radical and I love that word *radical* because it means going to the roots. This is the time for radical change. This is the time to come into our bodies and dance and drum and rise.

This is the time to stop apologizing for our belief in a world where everyone gets fed and taken care of, where we leave the rest of the oil in the ground, where those who do the hardest work are honored and paid the most, where we take our direction and inspiration from the most marginalized and invisible, where we trust our imaginations that once lined up in the direction of life will begin to create astounding and rapid solutions. Where we transform human suffering not by incarceration, policing, punishment, and degradation but by investigation into root causes. Where we stop celebrating royalty with money and fame as our models but instead honor and highlight those who humbly and without resources have transformed their communities. Where we trust the mystical, emotional, and erotic as much as we trust the intellectual and political and understand that their integration is not only the catalyst for revolution but may in fact be the revolution itself. Where we come to know that humility is the path to revolution and service the only song.

This is the time to come out of our silos, our movement ghettoes, and understand that each struggle for justice is a piece of the whole struggle, and rather than being cauterized and divided by hunger for resources and the spotlight, we give up dominion and fiercely and joyfully embrace the interconnectedness of every one of these things. There is no hierarchy of suffering, only the joining into a single river of outrage, compassion, and revolt. This is the time to remake the structure, to reclaim the original garden.

And remember the tree of life, the offering of apples/mushrooms was there inside the patriarchal garden, it has always been within us.

In the end it's about people, respect love honoring cherishing valuing life and people and our mother. We are Eve's children. Daughter of our Black African mother, Eve. Revolutionary, Eve, who ate the apple that unearthed the first garden under the imposed and constructed garden. Eve, who ate the apple as her hunger for truth was our actual path and now, we must fulfill her legacy.

Eve, mother of our freedom, ate the apple to liberate us into this world, our world. This is our time. Eat the fucking apple.

"Becoming Part of That Suffering and Dancing Country"

2017

This was a speech I gave at the invitation of Kimberlé Williams Crenshaw, at the African American Policy Forum's "Say Her Name: 20 Years of Intersectionality in Action" gala upon the honor of receiving the Virginia Durr Solidarity Award.

Every white person in this country is born into a racist world. The work is to unmake yourself, decolonize yourself, give your life fully to this project. And consciousness comes in stages, in layers. Strip one away, another appears. It's a deep and demanding project and it requires every bit of your being and devotion. Which is why I don't believe in allies. Ally implies I am helping you with your problem. The struggle to end racism is actually the problem of white people in the same way that ending violence against women is the problem of men. Turns out we don't rape ourselves. But another added injustice to the many injustices is that not only does racism undermine, devastate, destroy

Black people, but then they are made responsible for fixing it.

Solidarity implies it is all of our problem. That we are in this equally together. Allyship suggests distance and comfort.

Solidarity implies something more daring, more direct, more radical, more consuming, more committed. It means crossing lines, taking the struggle upon ourselves. It means throwing ourselves into the hard painful work of excavating the history embedded in our DNA.

There is something easy about being an ally. When the going gets tough you can step away. And there is something patronizing about it. It reminds me of tolerance. I despise the word *tolerance*. It implies that I am tolerating you, putting up with you. It puts me in the position of authority, the one who tolerates.

Tolerates implies an inside and an outside. Solidarity is a "bond of unity between individuals, united around a common goal or against a common enemy—racism." It's time now to put our white bodies on the line for the freedom of Black people—time to be willing to forfeit our privilege and status, time to admit the devastation of a racist ideology and framework. Time to stop criticizing the tactics or methods of revolutionary movements that rise with bravery, heart, vision, patience, and heroic kindness in response to the most grotesque atrocities, murders, degradations, terror, isolation, and exclusion. Nothing will change until we are willing to shut up and listen and serve, willing to stop making it about us: our feelings, our hurts, our guilt.

Can we own our selfishness and fear and need for comfort and our desperation for power? Can we give ourselves in service without directing or determining? Can we walk behind Black people or beside them? Can we allow ourselves to get close, real close, and rub up against the burning pain of those we have abused, enslaved, raped, incarcerated, shot, lynched, ignored, diminished, and degraded? As James Baldwin brilliantly wrote:

> The white man's unadmitted—and apparently, to him, unspeakable—private fears and longings are projected onto the Negro. The only way he can be released from the Negro's tyrannical power over him is to consent, in effect, to become black himself, to become a part of that suffering and dancing country that he now watches wistfully from the heights of his lonely power and, armed with spiritual traveler's checks, visits surreptitiously after dark.

Can we become part of that dancing and suffering country and not make Black people responsible for our guilt and neglect?

Can we stop punishing people we have harmed for reminding us we have harmed them? Can we be that honest, that generous, that vulnerable, that humble that we are able to freely provide support and kinship?

Can we serve without expecting to be worshipped? Can we stop issuing instructions and offer our bodies for action instead? Can we make this terrible wrong of racism the center of our thought and moral occupation?

The truth is we are as much sinew as we are symbol. Our whiteness is our skin color, but it's also a torn sheet draping the dead, a flag of privilege that will not surrender, a town called separateness and power. Our whiteness is the color of shame.

So, can we sit and be still for a minute and let the onerous truth and sorrow and history wash over us? Then, in that cataclysmic silence, when we have touched into the tidal wave of our responsibility, we will know what lengths we have to go,

what risks we will have to take to dismantle this mad hatred—
and how fiercely we will have to love to right this wrong.

Disruption

KINGSTON, NEW YORK, 2016

This was part of a yearlong writing dialogue with the eco-philosopher and writer Derrick Jensen.

In almost every conversation lately, when my friends are discussing the various destructive disasters befalling the world, someone inevitably says, "We're fucked." A strange laughter follows that feels a bit strained, then silence, then the lingering unspoken questions: Is it true? Are we fucked? Is it over? Has the die already been cast? It's a strange question. It feels like a postmodern mental exercise in survival, assuring ourselves of the world's end in order not to have to face the horror of our past and current actions. Relief and release that we won't have to deal with the myriad of sufferings and madness. A form of psychological cutting that both soothes and harms — psychic self-injury that begins as a defense against an overwhelming world and serves as a form of distancing and control. It's hard to tell whether the group or person asking the question truly believes we're fucked, but asking it enough almost ensures a collapse in the will to fight for change. There's some masochistic pleasure, too, as if by asking the question one had defied the onslaught of the terrible by accepting it before it happens.

I can't tell you how often in my life I've been "accused" of being idealistic. Accused of being naive, as if hope or enthusiasm were an indication of a deep lacking in intelligence, an insult to the all-knowing doomsayers who have the secret key to the future. But I'm neither an idealist or naive. I'm what I might call a passionate absurdist. I actually believe that struggling to change the world is to a large degree absurd. And I am, at the same time, wholly committed to this practice. I feel often as I resist and write and rise and march a collapse of faith in the very moment of my resistance, that any tiny action I might make or inspire others to make is like throwing a thimbleful of water on a forest fire.

I'm aware as I march through the streets of New York protesting police shootings of unarmed Black people or standing to resist fracking in the Bakken oil fields and the sexual violence in the man camps there, or rising and dancing against the U.S. imperialist wars, how easily this gesture can be ignored or erased by the powers that be. I also am terrorized to think how not struggling would change me. I think of Beckett, the terrain of despair in his plays and the characters who struggle to survive the despair in a world they will never comprehend. But the plays are always about that struggle. Beckett is neither sentimental nor nihilistic.

And it is here where I think we must live now, on the edge of incomprehensible madness, refusing to give up and refusing to pretend. Dancing on the precipice of annihilation while passionately encouraging and welcoming the new. This is most difficult in a country, in a system that has thoroughly indoctrinated in us a refusal to think, that communicates in sound bites, in idiotic, consumable brandable, reductionist absolutes. To be a passionate absurdist requires embracing ambiguity, insecurity, and it means looking at the predicament we are in head-on. It means leaping and assuming you will fall, dancing in the chaotic impossible passionate possible.

I think, then, that two things must be guiding us: one, that we can through radical collective envisioning and commitment transform our existence so that humans can remain and be in alliance with the earth; and two, that we have been given this gift, on loan for each of our lifetimes, of this precious earth that is our mandate to cherish and protect.

As for the first, we do not know anything absolutely. There are predictions that can inform us, but there are many variables. If the earth were our child and we were told that she had a crippling disease with only a 5 percent chance of recovery, would we bring the child home from the hospital and give up and sit and watch her die? Or would we do everything in our power to make sure we expanded that 5 percent and brought on a miracle by our love, creativity, urgent devotion.

So, what's in our way?

This paragraph in a recent article on the Intercept website about Mossville, a town in Louisiana that was poisoned by surrounding factories, jumped out at me.

> It's no surprise, then, that the story of chronic illness in the United States is one of private hardship. American society as a whole tends to reject the notion that toxins cause disease except in cases of acute, indisputable exposure. Accepting this requires the willful suspension of disbelief and the consent—conscious or not—to

bear whatever illnesses may come. Some people, like those in Mossville, resist, but most Americans, as in Westlake, go along.

They succumb to a subtle form of fear, not of disease but of disruption.

The majority of people of Mossville chose for many years to deny the toxic poisoning of factories surrounding their town rather than disrupt their livelihoods and lifestyles. They chose what appeared to be security over a deeper knowing that they were being slowly murdered.

This feels like the story of humans right now. We would rather die than disturb our daily comforts and habits. We would rather be poisoned or destroyed than have our lives disrupted.

So, we must learn the art and practice of disruption. We must release the tentacles of our false securities and interrupt the world as we know it. We must assume that anywhere we live or anything we are doing can change or disintegrate on a dime, and we must practice changing and letting it go. Living as if there were no future but the one we are creating. Nothing guaranteed but our willingness to live as pioneers of a new consciousness and way. We must become disrupters. Interrupting business as usual, taking stands that forfeit our acceptance or economic elevation, risking disapproval and controversy, participating in actions that loosen our grip on the suicidal givens and push the tyrants to fall.

"Is This the Moment?"

JULY, 2, 2022

This was written for the Guardian *after the Supreme Court's* Dobbs *decision to erase our bodily rights.*

How did you feel when it happened? When they came to take away the rights to our bodily autonomy? When they said twelve-year-old girls would be forced to carry to full-term, and then go through excruciating labor to deliver, babies with the faces of their rapists. When they legalized paying bounty hunters to pursue us for living in our own flesh and blood and wombs. When they believed that those of us who had given our lives to be free, to walk our own paths and dream our most vital dreams, would easily and quietly surrender to their twisted cage, unable to see they were connected to other cages inside cages, each one taking more of our air and our light. I heard a shrieking, high-pitched laugh-scream coming out of my frothing, ancient mouth, my white hair blazing with fury. I wanted to weep and howl, and I did, for the depth of their hatred for me, for women, for Black women and brown women and Indigenous women and Asian women and young victims of incest and poor women and trans men and nonbinary birthers of babies and all the rest of us trying to get free.

So I wrote. I wrote and I wrote. I wrote piece after piece trying to say something smart. Something that hadn't been said. Something so revelatory and earth-shattering it would unlock the story, solve the crime, catalyze the opening. Finding the words that would undo this nightmare. That would save the young women and people who would die trying not to give birth and the ones who would be forever emotionally, economically, spiritually tortured and destroyed by having babies they never wanted, which would rob them of their dreams and destinies.

Words and poems that would, through the genius arrangement of syllables and rhythms and facts, historical references and metaphor, finally break the spell, the centuries-old curse of patriarchy: word dares, simple words, clear fucking words like no no no no no. We are never ever going back because we all know that once we agree to that we will open the door and they will come for everything and everyone.

In one of the pieces, I wrote a declaration of refusal. I refuse, I wrote. My conscience will not permit me to agree to the scornful decisions of a fringe minority on the Supreme Court—some of whom have been accused of sexual assault—appointed by a president who is a self-confessed perpetrator, those masquerading as judges to determine what goes on in this body or the precious, glorious, generous, life-giving, caring bodies of my sisters, whom I love with every fiber of my being.

But then I realized I wasn't sure how exactly we would refuse, what form that would take in a country with 400 million guns.

So here's what I know. I will not ever accept this decision to go back against myself, my body, and all the years of our bloodily fought-for freedoms. I know there are multitudes who feel the same. I don't have the answers but I have questions. I believe in questions.

Will we be passive, obedient followers of unjust laws? Will we be more concerned with formality than justice, acquiesce to corrupt and delegitimized institutions — rather than devotion to conscience and each other?

Will the magnitude of our joining forces catalyze our imaginations, our ferocity, and solidarity, and emerge with a collective vision — a series of surprising, successful actions?

Will we finally agree to understand that the struggle for abortion rights is the struggle against white supremacy, is the struggle to end gender oppression and patriarchy, so that we stand by each other when they come to each of our doors?

Will we finally be able to release our self-delusions, which have obscured the Supreme Court's historically racist and inherently patriarchal practices, and stop turning our lives and will over to these institutions run mainly by white men who work against the majority, the vulnerable and oppressed?

Will we trust our bodies and defend their sovereignty against church and state?

Will this be the moment when we finally come to celebrate that not one of us has the answer or will ever write the definitive piece, but when we choose to line up side by side in the same direction with the uniqueness each of us has to offer, the way forward will be revealed?

Is this the moment we've been waiting for?

Is it called Revolution?

Could it happen with love?

I offer you my hand.

Then We Were Jumping

SPONGANO, ITALY, 2013

In the dream he comes
and sits across from me
at something that resembles a table
but it has the constellation of
the stars painted on the top of it
He is wearing his old yellow sweater
the one he only wore in the house
He looks uneasy
older than I remember
and sad
I remember this sadness
I lived in this sadness
Like a fog,
Like a virus
I gave my body to him
To make this sadness go away
And when that didn't work
he decided to make me as sad as him.

But here now at the table with the stars
And the falling galaxy that seems to
come alive and twinkle between us
I know surely that this sadness belongs to him
and for the first time
I don't move
Away or toward
I don't move at all
I feel strangely confident
I look up and realize
There is a vast circle
Of people sitting around us
And we are in something like
a coliseum
and people are patient and quietly waiting
some women are knitting potholders
and others are slightly waving red flags
a few men are leaning forward in their seats
smoking cigarettes
some are wearing strange whimsical hats
They are not the kind of people
my father would have talked to
and they know this
but they are not unkind
My father suddenly gets annoyed
the way he used to get
impatient and he says with a mean face,
"What are you looking for, Evie?"
He seems so fragile
But I know I am not meant to save him
and then this silence

descends
a jar of liquid
light
around us
holding us, containing us
and out of nowhere
this blob, this dirty bloody transparent blob
filled with sharp noises and crumbs of cruelty
starts coming out of me
out of all the parts of my body
pouring out of me
gathering
into one huge blob
and it floats like a bloody rain cloud
hovering over my father's head
like it is expecting something
and my father takes a beat
looks up
and then he just opens his mouth
so natural so easy
very wide his mouth
and he receives my pain
swallows it whole
and all the people start cheering
I watch my father
so full
his cheeks bulging and red
almost about to explode
not able to take much more
and then these red tears begin to
pour down my father's cheeks

I'm a little scared
because it looks like he's crying blood
But the people are still cheering
They are encouraging
This goes on for a while
My father crying blood red tears
And then as I am looking
My father suddenly becomes younger
and younger until
he's a little boy
and he isn't
sad
he is dazzling and clever
and playful
he takes me by the hand
and walks me out into the center
of the coliseum which is
now a field of wild high ticklish grass
blowing in an almost hysterical wind
and we just start jumping and jumping
crazy jumping
I can't believe how high we are jumping
It's like the earth has become a trampoline
And I am not afraid now to jump higher and higher
When I wake up, I think
 Oh, this is justice.

EPILOGUE

V: A Dream Vision of
My New Name

*I have taken V now as my name. The name I was originally given
was connected to the one who attempted to destroy and undo me.
V is my freedom name.*

I come from the V.

I didn't always know this. One of the things the Extractors
took from me, from us, was memory. They buried it and terrorized it out of us. First, they made us mock our mothers, then
they made us forget them and our language and our names.
They made us forget our very particular ways. Their violence
separated us from our bodies and because our bodies housed our
energy, our knowing, our intuition, our sexuality, we became
separated from all that made us who we were.

V is the name of my real people and reminder of my true
origins. It was only by releasing the one who had violated me
that I was able to begin to remember. He was assigned the role
of my father. For almost sixty years, even long after he died, he
occupied me with terror and made me ignorant and dumb.

Now, since the exorcism, much of my memory is returning. Now through the workings of plant medicines and the whispering of trees my original ancestors begin to speak to me. The Extractors brought something called trauma. It seems to have infiltrated every person and everything, even our precious earth. It is a ravaging and all-encompassing injury, a shattering that if not made whole will break us further and cause more breaks in others. It makes us afraid and paranoid and hurt. It turns us against ourselves.

I want you to know where I come from and I want you to know about my people. Many of them live in the walls of the rooms of your houses, in your dreams. The V were a vast and humble people. V for Vessel, opening, invitation, the upward reaching side of a diamond, inviting the downward side for completion. My people prayed with their arms outstretched in a V. The Divine met the V and in that diamond completion, there was a luminous fusion, messages, wisdom, were transmitted through the V connector into the people.

In the V community there was no such thing as hierarchy: no one above and no one below. There was no one more important and no one less important. Each person had a particular gift, an offering to the community, and sometimes those gifts evolved and changed. All gifts were valued equally. Each child was encouraged to follow their bliss because that would evolve their particular gift. Some children could speak to birds and communicate with trees. Some were precocious and drew images of things they could not have seen in their short years. Some saw the future. They had the gift of prophecy.

Sometimes the longing for my origins comes as a sharp unrelenting pain. I don't know if I am longing for a place, another realm, a time, or a planet even. I have tried to explain to those I love that when I say that I want to go home, I do not feel suicidal. I feel homesick for the place of V.

From the second I was born, earthly ways deeply confused me. The harsh birth experience in bright lights, my mother totally numb to me, her lying flat on her back as if someone had pressed and caught her there. I tried for so many years to get her to come back to me.

There were so many disturbing things about this place. I loved so many people as a child, well to be honest, I loved everyone. I was constantly reprimanded for this, told it was not possible to love this many people. Told I must be insincere or fake. I was instructed to be discerning and selective in my loving. I was punished early on for being too emotional, too available, and too sexual. I did not understand how anyone could be too much of any of those things.

The V were brought up to believe that the expansion of our ability to feel and our life force was the point of our existence. We lived in constant touch, constant pleasure, there was no such thing as work, as everything we did was endowed with enjoyment. It's funny that now they call people who crave pleasure *hedonist* like it's an insult or an indulgence or a sickness rather than the point of life. Back then our plan was to make everyone as safe and happy and cherished as possible. We went to school to learn how to do this. We studied with great teachers. We learned to listen, we learned to be constantly self-evaluating, we learned to ask questions, we learned the art of apology, as of course each of us was only human and would constantly make mistakes that might inadvertently hurt someone. There were some who became masters of apology. They evolved a humility that was awe-inspiring.

All of the V took care of one another. There was no I or me.

And although that may sound frightening to those of you who have built your existence on the basis of yourself, the WE is where the pleasure lived. The WE / the double V was the center of the expansion.

Everything they did was in alignment with this. How they farmed and grew their food, how they built their homes, how they shared their water and kept it clean and flowing, how they designed their communities, all of it simultaneously expanding their ability to connect and to cherish one another and life.

So, you can imagine how very beautiful it was. They were taught early that developing the capacity to see the beauty of their planet was the first critical step of expanding consciousness, and then they were trained to follow that by learning to imitate and manifest that beauty in everything they made or did—how they dressed, how they decorated their homes. Our whole planet was essentially an altar, bodies were altars, each one of their homes was an altar too. They designed platforms and places to worship, to connect and invite their spirit guides. They spent their days making offerings to the divine outside, inside, and in one another. Making things beautiful was the highest calling. There was no limit to the time one could spend on this because there was no notion of time. Beginnings and endings were what the Extractors brought because everything they did was about limitation and control. The V's intention was simply to deepen the ability of their bodies and beings to feel and know and expand into presence and ecstasy. To know it and receive this energy and become it and proliferate it. Anything in the way of that had to be removed or transformed or burned away in themselves. Sometimes they had carried fragments of pain or karma from other worlds or lifetimes or ancestors or dreams that did not belong in their world.

The Extractors created an inside and an outside. An up and a down. Before, the V lived in one ocean of gathering, in one breath of being. They lived as an ever-widening, ever-expanding WE. The V was the reminder of this opening. They learned at an early age that nature was kin and that if they slowed everything down, if they devoted themselves to the practice of presence, which involved attention, detailed attention to everything around them—trees and moss and lichen and mycelium and dew and ducks—they could begin to feel what was inside them. Once this happened, they would know them and be them, and forever protect them as they would be one with them. They learned that the way to merge or feel the natural world was to imitate it or portray or examine it through art and theater and music and literature and science and understanding.

Sexuality was what activated the world of the grown-ups. There was nothing shameful about it. It was the highest energy. It was worshipped, as it was the vibration that kept them forever connected to the divine. Sexuality was divine. Masturbation was the highest form of prayer. Many of them were very practiced at it. To know your own sexual rhythms and intensities, to ride them and learn to direct and open them without harming or invading was the highest art and good. When the Extractors came, they were disturbed by the V's openness and intensity. Something terrible had clearly already happened to the Extractors, and they were ragged and closed and mean. The unapologetic ecstasy of the V enraged them and made them feel jealous and inferior. They read their invitation as a way of mocking them rather than as a way of joining them. This set them on a terrible course against the V. They began a ruthless campaign to diminish and reduce them. They raped and maimed and murdered their sacred bodies.

The V had never known these horrors, so they were particularly vulnerable. The Extractors brought a thing called shame. It was a poison. They covered the V with it and soaked them in it and injected it into their bloodstream. This was even worse than the violence because after a time the V could no longer distinguish the shame from their original selves. It became them. Shameful them. This shame made them doubt and diminish their life force. They began to hate their own essence. The religious masters of the Extractors indoctrinated the V in something called sin, and through this the Extractors began to erase the V's vibrancy and brilliance. The V stopped being visible, as they did not want to attract more violent attention. They began to hide themselves. Like the cicadas they went underground, into their private human caves. They rarely saw one another or the sun. They lost their WE. Once they lost this power, the Extractors were able to take complete control.

They brought shame to the V's genitals. They separated them out from the rest of their bodies. The Extractors separated the V into genders, into races, binaries that would eventually come to war with each other. Each division was shocking and catastrophic because they had been a people who found their meaning in the joining. They had no protection against this demonic dividing. One division created other divisions, cancers mutating into other cancers. Once that process had begun there was no way to stop it.

Before, the adult V had never known something called sex. Everything was about developing one's capacity for aliveness and pleasure, soothing, excitement and connection. After the Extractors came, sex was separated out just like the genitals. But before, every part of the body was a portal that had orgasmic potential. Genitals were the most obvious, but the most experienced and devoted of them could orgasm just by rubbing their ears or touching the inside of their ankles. The V spent their days developing this ability. And often they spent their days in group pleasure. The more the merrier. They learned to undulate as one. This undulation of thousands of bodies in unison became a vibrational field or force that allowed those who served as V bridges or V connectors to bring the energy of the community to meet the energy of the divine in the fusion diamond. Those who were gifted with the ability to be *connectors* were those who had freed their bodies from any blockages resulting from fear or ego. They had given their lives to becoming conduits, developing their strength to expand and release into the powerful energies moving in both directions. They were equivalent to Olympic athletes, but they were High Priests and Priestesses.

Every three months the V had weeklong ceremonies where the whole adult community first bathed in their natural springs, then oiled themselves so they were fluid and free, then arranged themselves as a single human instrument, lying side by side, in various formations, naked on the earth in the north field of silky moss. Musicians played ecstatic music that encouraged and lubricated their movements and escalated their undulations, pushing them into this wild and most invigorating energetic exchange. It was in the fine weave of their synchronicity that each of them was born into their power. They did not feel less special by the melding of their individual egos, they felt relieved and released into the bliss of the ever expanding. And it was during these ceremonies that their blessed connectors brought in the messages, the wisdom, the counsel from the divine or their highest selves. All their living principles came from these rituals, their guiding laws and commitments to one another. They were never questioned or disputed, as everyone had been part of their creation and delivery.

Here in this particular time of trauma, where the individual is worshipped and held before all else, we see the great hardship it has caused. In the time of the V they did not have such things as factories, huge farms, banks, prisons, money, police, nation-states, soldiers, credit cards, bureaucracy, warehouses, anything that numbed people or treated them or made them feel less than human or took them out of their bodies or hurt their bodies. They did not know marriage or any kinds of coupling that involved ownership or separation from the rest of the community.

They did not know punishment, abandonment, exclusion, deprivation, war, cruelty, poverty, grades, reviews, disability, elites, racism that would have implied that they were not one race. Their pleasure was based on the stunning beauty of diversity among and within them. Jealousy was a rare occurrence because everyone felt seen and held by everyone. Each one of them knew for certain that they were one of her creations. How could they not love each other and themselves, how could they ever determine that one of them was better or more right than another or not worthy of love. That would have been the greatest insult to their creator. Each person arrived with physical, emotional, and psychological particularities that were teachings for both the person and the whole community. If a person was depressed, for example, they were considered a gift, developing the layers of patience, and care. If someone was born blind, they deepened and refined the community's sense of touch, smell, sound, and sensuality. The joy of existence was learning how to serve each person's emotional and physical particularities.

I have never written about the V before. First, it took most of my life to be strong enough to tolerate the unbearable intensity of remembering. For in the memory was the grief of what was lost. In the memory was the sorrow of the cruelty. In the memory was and is the rage at the futile stupidity of the violent.

I have been afraid to share what I remember. I know how cynical and judgmental this world can be. I have been hurt over and over by the cold suspicion of the untreated ones who are bleeding and brutal. Their scoffing nearly crushed me as child. And, when I was fifty-five, the accumulated pain of cruelty became too much.

Instead of making life, my womb swelled a lump of death. It grew and grew and broke through the mother wall and quickly began to seize other parts of my body.

Through the combined powers of Western medicine and the healing properties of holy love, through the shamanic practices of burning away injuries, lies, traumatic wounds, distortions, and bad choices, I was birthed back to the trees, the dirt, the stars, the sun, and most dramatically back into my own body. That's where the memories were stored, and some were released upon entry. But still something kept me from opening the rest.

It was only when I became strong enough to climb into the soul of my father predator, only when I was able to understand who he was and why, only when I allowed myself to be gripped mercilessly by his unfelt agony, only when I was able to detail his crimes toward me, and only after I wrote his in-depth apology that I was finally able to release the Extractors' grip on me.

"Change your name," a voice said shortly after. "Take the name of your first family, V."

You will of course have your doubts and derisions. "By what authority?" "What proof?" "How can we be sure the V ever existed?"

The whole world is a story of somebody's making. Those

with the power get to determine the characters, the angles, and the shape. I believe in the power of a name—a testament or an honoring, a recalling or a conjuring. What might seem like a memory can as surely be a prophecy.

It's up to us. Up to us.

ACKNOWLEDGMENTS

To all those who helped *Reckoning* come to be:

I am totally indebted to Paula Allen, who spent months poring over piles of journals, stacks of articles, and literary magazines to help identify work for this book. *Reckoning* would not have been possible without you. I am thrilled to have your magnificent images throughout these pages as they have moved throughout my life. I celebrate our sisterhood and our many years of travel together across this broken, miraculous planet.

Thank you to my editor, Nancy Miller, for your belief in this book from the beginning, for your insights and brilliant editorial notes, for your endless encouragement.

Bless you, Charlotte Sheedy, for over forty-five years. I can't imagine what my life as a writer would have been without you. You are simply the most visionary, devoted, loving, consistent, intrepid champion and friend a writer could ever have.

Thank you, Tony Montenieri, for your thorough and brilliant support that made this book possible. You are simply the best.

Thank you, Susan Celia Swan, Purva Panday Cullman, Rada Boric, Johann Hari, Alnoor Ladha, Cecilie Surasky, Alixa García, Alia Lahlou, Carole Black, Jennifer Buffett, Pat Mitchell, Jane Fonda, Nicoletta Billi, Sue Grand, Diana

DeVegh, Zillah Eisenstein, Nancy Rose, and George Lane for your time, insights, questions on the manuscript, and for your magnificent hearts.

Thank you, Naomi Klein, for the gorgeous back cover photo and for all the amazing talks that led to this book.

Thank you to Katharine Viner and all those at the *Guardian* who gave me a home for new ideas.

As this book contains writing from the last forty-five years of my life, I bow to my dear friends, collaborators, and comrades, my sisters in the movement, my lovers, my ancestors, all those who published pieces at earlier times, and all those who have inspired, supported, and challenged me across time, particularly James Baldwin, Samuel Beckett, Toni Morrison, Muhammad Ali, and sister of my heart, Arundhati Roy.

Thank you to Christine Schuler Deschryver and Dr. Denis Mukwege for the most profound work, love, collaboration, and journey in the Democratic Republic of the Congo.

Thank you, beloved Monique Wilson, for the depth of our sisterhood and for all those late nights from Manila to Kingston during the plague.

Bless you, Celeste Lecesne, my sister/brother, for our life at Lotus Pond Farm, where this book was born, for those healing leg rubs, for the depth of your faith in my work, and for your magic.

For Dylan, Coco, and Niko—how lucky, how blessed am I to call you family.

PHOTO CREDITS

TEXT CREDITS

A NOTE ON THE AUTHOR

V (formerly Eve Ensler) is a Tony Award–winning playwright, author, performer, and activist. Her many plays include the Obie Award–winning and international phenomenon *The Vagina Monologues*, which has been translated into 48 languages and performed in more than 140 countries. She is the author of a number of books, including her latest best-sellers, *The Apology*, now translated into twenty languages, and *In the Body of the World*, as well the *New York Times* bestseller *I Am an Emotional Creature*. She starred on Broadway in *The Good Body* and most recently Off Broadway at Manhattan Theater Club in the critically acclaimed *In the Body of the World*. She wrote the story and co-wrote the lyrics for *WILD: A Music Becoming* that premiered at American Repertory Theater in 2021. She is the founder of V-Day, the twenty-five-year-old global activist movement that has raised over 120 million dollars to end violence against all (cisgender, transgender, and gen-der-diverse) women and girls and the planet and One Billion Rising, the largest global mass action to end gender-based vio-lence in over 200 countries. She is a cofounder of the City of Joy, a revolutionary center for women survivors of violence in the Democratic Republic of the Congo, along with Christine

Schuler Deschryver and Dr. Denis Mukwege, winner of the 2018 Nobel Peace Prize. She is one of Newsweek's "150 Women Who Changed the World" and the Guardian's "100 Most Influential Women." She writes regularly for the Guardian. She lives in New York.

Also available from V (formerly Eve Ensler):

The Apology

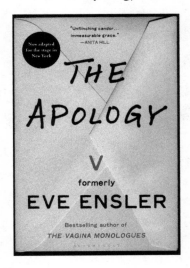

From the bestselling author of *The Vagina Monologues*—a powerful, life-changing examination of abuse and atonement.

Like millions of women, V has been waiting much of her lifetime for an apology. Sexually and physically abused by her father, V has struggled her whole life from this betrayal, longing for an honest reckoning from a man who is long dead. After years of work as an anti-violence activist, she decided she would wait no longer; an apology could be imagined, by her, for her, to her. *The Apology*, written by V from her father's point of view in the words she longed to hear, attempts to transform the abuse she suffered with unflinching truthfulness, compassion, and an expansive vision for the future.

Remarkable and original, *The Apology* is an acutely transformational look at how, from the wounds of sexual abuse, we can begin to re-emerge and heal. It is revolutionary, asking everything of each of us: courage, honesty, and forgiveness.

"For those men—the famous and the unknown—*The Apology* is a blueprint of contrition." –Ron Charles, *The Washington Post*

"A remarkable book." –Brian Lehrer, WNYC

"A triumph of artistry and empathy." –Naomi Klein

"A crucial step forward… This is an urgently needed book right now." –Jane Fonda